GREATER IN EUROPE

GREATER IN EUROPE

by

BILL NEWTON DUNN
*Member of the European Parliament
for Lincolnshire and North-East Nottinghamshire*

Regency Press (London & New York) Ltd.
125 High Holborn, London WC1V 6QA

Copyright © 1985 by W. F. Newton Dunn

This book is copyrighted under the Berne Convention. No portion may be reproduced by any process without the copyright holder's written permission except for the purposes of reviewing or criticism, as permitted under the Copyright Act of 1956.

ISBN 0 7212 0731 6

Printed and bound in Great Britain by
Buckland Press Ltd., Dover, Kent.

CONTENTS

Chapter		Page
1	Could The British Afford To Leave The Community Now?	7
2	The True Choice Now Facing The British People	17
3	The March To European Unity Since 1946	24
4	But Where Are Our Benefits So Far?	35
5	An Alarming Gap In Democratic Control	50
6	Next Steps In The Community's Development?	55
7	Sovereignty, The Misunderstood Concept	63
8	We Could Get Much More Out Of The Community	68
9	Who Is Afraid Of A United States Of Europe?	81
	Index	83

CHAPTER ONE

Could the British Afford to Leave the Community Now?

It was as long ago as January 1973 that the United Kingdom joined the European Community. But our role in the Community is still debated these many years later. As each year passes our involvement in Europe has increased and the price of disentanglement has grown.

The arguments have now become exceedingly strong that we should remain *inside* the European Community.

The major reasons why we must stay in are:

a. The Common Market is now by far Britain's biggest customer, taking more than forty per cent of all our exports. If we were outside, our automatic access to the market would no longer be guaranteed.

b. The British point of view about European trading rules and future European development is only taken fully into account while we are members of the Community.

c. Our political interests vis-a-vis rest of the world coincide increasingly with those of the other European Community countries.

d. The expense of supporting British agriculture would be greater if we were outside the Community.

e. The British people possess enlarged rights and freedoms which they would not have outside the Community—the freedoms to work and to live wherever they choose in eleven other countries in western Europe.

To retain these very important advantages, the British *must* remain inside the European Community.

IF WE LEFT THE COMMUNITY...

If we were to leave, barriers would gradually be put up against our most successful exports to Europe which we could not easily overcome; the opinions of fifty-five million British concerning world affairs would be isolated instead of being supported by the other two hundred and seventy million Europeans; we would have to pay higher taxes to support our farmers who grow our food; we would not have the legal right to work and to settle in other European countries.

Nobody has offered an alternative plan for the British which would restore us these advantages. Opponents of our membership are never able to explain convincingly where else we could turn to obtain the same benefits. They cannot do so, because there is nowhere else. The Labour Party talks about a "fortress Britain", with more planning and more controls. But this is patently absurd because we have always been a great trading people, earning our living by exploration, travel and trade.

BRITAIN'S EXPORTERS NEED THE COMMON MARKET
None of the major political parties in Britain disputes that we need the continent's markets for our exports. Over forty per cent—approaching one half—of all our exports go directly into the Common Market; another twenty per cent go to the Free Trade Area countries of Europe which include Norway, Sweden, Switzerland, Austria and Finland. There is no alternative market of similar size for us. The Communist bloc in eastern Europe is smaller and much less prosperous as well as being politically very unattractive. The United States of America are distant and probably too competitive. The Commonwealth has altered in recent years with many of its members now having found closer and richer markets such as Japan and the U.S.A.

Ill-informed critics of the Community suggest that a major part of the forty per cent of our exports that go straight into the Common Market countries is merely British oil. But the actual share of the forty per cent which is oil is only four per cent: oil is a valuable but only small part of our exports. Indeed, if we had no oil to export, it is very probable that our exports to Europe would be even higher than they already are—because oil has made the British currency higher priced than it would otherwise be with a consequent disadvantage to our exporters.

Nor would it be enough for the British to try to export into continental markets "at arms length" from outside the Community. We discovered that was a mistake very soon after we had boycotted the founding of the Common Market in 1957, and therefore we very soon applied to join in 1961. Probably one reason why British motorcar manufacturers have shrunk so much, while the French, German and Italian car makers have remained large, is that our government refused to join the Common Market when theirs did in 1957.

The difference between being inside and being outside the Community is the difference between having a say in making the rules which affect us against having no say in making the rules but still having to follow them.

Whether we leave or not, the European Community will continue to exist and to develop. It will continue to be the most important and influential body in our corner of the world, whose decisions it will be impossible to ignore. It would therefore be wiser to stay inside and to have a voice in the decisions rather than leaving and waiting to be told about them afterwards.

Nor can critics of our membership argue successfully that the continentals need our British market more than we need theirs. The other member states' exports to us are only some fifteen per cent of their total exports, whereas we depend on them for over forty per cent of ours.

In fact, the British have a greater need for freedom to export successfully than has any other industrialised country in the world. We export a higher proportion of our Gross National Product, over thirty per cent, than anyone else! Compared with our thirty per cent, the Americans export about ten per cent, the Japanese about twelve per cent, the French and the Germans around twenty four per cent of their own Gross National Products. As champion exporters, it is vital for Britain to have guaranteed access to continental markets.

Critics of the Community suggest that the decline in Britain's manufacturing industries is caused by our membership. Unfortunately the painful truth is that we have a growing trade deficit in manufactured goods with both Community and with non-Community industrial countries. The true reason for the overall decline of British manufacturing industries is our own lack of competitiveness. That is own fault and not the fault of our neighbours. If we cannot compete successfully in our nearest market on the continent and where there are no tariffs to hinder us, we are very unlikely to succeed any better in more distant markets.

OUR POLITICAL INTERESTS INCREASINGLY COINCIDE WITH THE CONTINENT'S

In our policies towards the rest of the world, our interests and those of our continental neighbours are becoming increasingly similar.

Compared with either of the two superpowers, all the separate nations of western Europe are small. The opinion of each European country, if voiced separately and in its own way, carries little weight with the rest of the world. But when all the countries of the European Community speak with a single united voice in foreign affairs —as happens increasingly—expressing the views of nearly three hundred million people, there is a considerably greater impact on world opinion.

Foreign and international affairs are hardly ever debated in British General Elections any more, such matters being tactily acknowledged as increasingly beyond the control of a national parliament such as Westminster.

Similarly, Europe's efforts to aid the underdeveloped countries are more effective if they are co-ordinated. All Europeans share an interest in seeing underdeveloped countries become prosperous—not only because all human beings are equally entitled to prosper, but also because Europe, being in decline demographically and technologically and having few raw materials of its own, will increasingly need their friendship.

Again, in the search for new jobs, new industries and new technologies which we have to find in order to replace our declining traditional industries, our best chance is to co-operate together with other member countries of the Community—rather than each country researching the same limited amount of ground by itself with its own limited resources. Otherwise the Americans and the Japanese, who each have much larger home markets than any single European country, will win the competition to develop new technologies and industries, so leaving Europeans to suffer from higher unemployment, lower standards of living, or dependance on the superpowers.

AGRICULTURE WOULD COST THE BRITISH TAX PAYER MORE OUTSIDE THE COMMUNITY

The Common Agricultural Policy (known as the "C.A.P.") has been a popular target for criticism in Britain. We lost our chance to have more favourable rules when we refused to join at the founding of the European Community in 1957. The C.A.P. costs Britain money because we have fewer farmers than the other member states. This was understood and accepted by our negotiators when we joined in 1973. It was hoped—too optimistically as it turns out—that in return for the cost of agriculture, many continentals would be buying British factory made products and would take to driving British-made motorcars.

THE SUCCESS OF THE COMMON AGRICULTURAL POLICY

The Common Agricultural Policy has been a great *success*, contrary to the popular criticism which it receives in Britain. Its rules were drawn up—in the voluntary absence of the British—with two major objectives.

One objective of the C.A.P. was to encourage food production in western Europe, at a time when memories of food rationing were still recent. The idea that we might one day achieve self-sufficiency in food or even have surpluses seemed like a distant dream.

The second major objective of the C.A.P. was to assist smallscale farmers on the continent to modernise. There had been very great fragmentation of farms and land-holdings due to Napoleon's insistence that possessions including farmlands must be divided *equally* among all one's children. The C.A.P. has proved to be a very great success in altering this. There has been a great improvement in agricultural efficiency on the continent. It is said that for every minute that Britain has been in the Community since 1973, one person in France has stopped working in agriculture. When Britain joined in 1973, eighteen per cent of the French worked on the land: now the proportion is only nine per cent! Much still remains to be achieved, particularly in the more backward Mediterranean areas of Greece, southern Italy, Spain and Portugal.

Now at last, production has expanded so that there are surpluses of food which are too large. It is time for adjustments to the rules of the Common Agricultural Policy. But the necessary adjustments must not be made in the last minute way that milk quotas were imposed upon dairy farmers by the Council of Ministers in March 1984 after their several years of reluctance to face up to and accept the need for change. No national minister from any member state should be allowed to mislead his farmers by arguing for a *right* to self-sufficiency in any product: if every country claimed a right to self-sufficiency there would be no common market.

It is utterly unrealistic for British critics of the C.A.P. to call unilaterally for wholesale changes to the Common Agricultural Policy. To make changes would mean first winning the consent of all the other Community member states—and they show no signs of being interested in dramatic wholesale changes. Nor could Britain withdraw from the C.A.P. separately with out also withdrawing from the European Community altogether.

If Britain left the Community, more than one expert has calculated that in order to maintain the standards of British agriculture by paying direct subsidies it would cost the British taxpayer around an extra one and a half billion pounds per year in increased taxation. That equals an increase in tax of thirty pounds per year for every man, woman and child in the country. It would thus be very expensive for British taxpayers to withdraw from the Community.

As an alternative to paying extra tax in order to keep up our agriculture outside the Community, the British could choose instead to reduce the level of support paid to farmers. However this would cause the level of production of food in Britain to decline. We would then have to pay to import more food so that our balance of payments would suffer adversely.

It is unrealistic to try to end all support to our farmers. Because of the unpredictability of the weather from one year to the next, every country in the world finds it necessary to support its own agriculture. Since 1981, the U.S.A.'s support for American farmers have far exceeded European support in the same period: in 1983 the European Community spent around sixteen billion dollars on the C.A.P., whereas American agriculture was subsidised by around nineteen billion dollars plus another nine and a half billion dollars for their payments-in-kind programme.

Could we British rely on buying food more cheaply from world surpluses instead of from the continent of Europe? This is a popular idea in Britain, but it would prove unsatisfactory for two major reasons. First, most of the world's surpluses are small in comparison to Britain's needs: if we became a major buyer on world markets, we would force up the prices. Second, world surpluses are temporary from one year to the next: in years of shortage or of famine we would have to buy at peak prices or go without—to the intense dislike of the British shopper who profers stability, both of supply and of price.

Food prices in Britain have actually decreased—in real terms—since we joined the Community in 1973. Some foods have become dearer, others much cheaper. Since 1973 the retail price index in Britain has increased by slightly more than has our food price index over the same period.

In the longer term the world's population is growing very rapidly—from four billion today to a forecast six billion by the year 2000. We would be very unwise to rely on always being able to find plentiful cheap food on world markets. Sadly, we must recognise that in many parts of the world in the coming decade famines are at least as probable as surpluses.

It should be explained that Europe's food surpluses—mainly butter, beef and cereals—do not belong to the European Community, but they belong to the national government of the country where they are stored. The Community only pays for the storage and for the final disposal costs if a subsidy is necessary. It is the national government which pays the farmer and which owns the surpluses. Therefore in a situation such as the Ethiopian famine, the ability to donate the surpluses rests in the hands of national governments, both because they own the surpluses and because they each have far greater financial resources than does the European Community.

OUR INDIVIDUAL FREEDOMS WOULD SHRINK IF WE LEFT THE COMMUNITY

Conservative philosophy is to obtain the maximum amount of freedom and of choice for the British people. The long term objective for the Community is that we shall enjoy the freedoms we now have in Britain but multiplied many times because they are throughout the twelve member states.

Increasingly, young people are taking advantage of the rights conferred on them by the Treaty of Rome—that they can travel, live and work wherever they choose in the European Community. For Britain to leave the Community would be to limit the freedoms which are already guaranteed to our youngsters, a most un-Conservative step to take.

WE WOULD FORFEIT FOREIGN INVESTMENT IN BRITAIN IF WE LEFT

If we left the Community, we would forefeit future Japanese and American investment in new factories and jobs because they see us as a way into the Common Market. Britain has received the greatest share of American and Japanese investment in Europe since we joined the Community in 1973.

OTHER DAMAGING CONSEQUENCES OF LEAVING THE COMMUNITY

If we left, we should not be able to demand fair treatment from our previous partners in the Community: in addition they might wish to make sure that the penalties for withdrawal were sufficiently severe in order to discourage any other waverers.

If the unhoped-for event ever happened whereby the Labour Party ever regained sole power in Britain, they would unilaterally give up our nuclear defences. We should then expect to be forced to give up our veto in the Security Council of the United Nations, as happened previously to Taiwan. It might be only a very small consolation to see our veto given to the Community instead.

If we left, we would become a true offshore island—increasingly out of the mainstream of events, increasingly less important to the rest of the world, increasingly protected from the competitive pressures which now oblige us to modernise, increasingly clinging instead to old institutions, old assets and old attitudes. We should become a cork bobbing loose in waves created by the major world powers including the Community. Our sovereignty would become nearer to that of Liechtenstein rather than the sovereignty of the major power which we aspire to be. All major decisions would be taken for us by our powerful neighbours.

It is hard to believe that an isolated Britain, with its noted reluctance to adapt in a fast-changing world, would modernise itself sufficiently to keep up with the rest of the world. It seems more likely that Britain would become like an elderly crotchety retired admiral; proud, increasingly poor, and living on glorious memories of the past. That is not an outcome that any Conservative desires for future generations of Britons.

As our oil surplus slowly runs out, we shall become increasingly poor relative to the other member states. Even now we stand only seventh in prosperity in the Community. By remaining inside we may be able to share their future prosperity—including social benefits. We may gain other benefits too: if trade union legislation were to be harmonised throughout the Community, British unions would lose their outdated immunities from the law and would be obliged by competitive pressures from the continent to abandon their antiquarian labour rigidities in Britain.

"BUT SOME OTHER EUROPEAN COUNTRIES SURVIVE ON THEIR OWN"

Critics of our membership suggest that Britain should be able to survive on its own just as a number of small European states do today. But the situation of each of those countries is unique, and none provides a suitable parallel for Britain. It is instructive to examine briefly why.

SPAIN AND PORTUGAL
Both these countries have recently joined the Community, having become democratic after long intervals. Clearly, both believed that it was better to be inside the Community rather than outside.

NORWAY
The Norwegians are oil rich and do not depend on selling a large volume of industrial exports. They negotiated to join the Community in 1973 at the same time as the British, the Irish and the Danes. After their government had completed negotiations successfully, they held a referendum of the Norwegian people. A rumour spread that if Norway joined, the foreigners could take away their new found oil. This was a false rumour, as the British now know. However, the Norwegian people voted narrowly by fifty-three to forty-seven per cent not to join the Community. Now the Norwegians have to follow the Community's decisions about trade without having a say in them. It is possible to forsee that the time may come when Norway may re-apply to join in order to obtain a say in European decision making.

SWEDEN
Sweden has been neutral militarily for three hundred years. Predominantly with a socialist government, it has viewed the joining of the European Community as a politically biased act which would upset its powerful eastern neighbour, the Soviet Union. However there is frustration that the Community takes the Swedish point of view insufficiently into account when deciding rules for European trade. If the Russians continue to violate Swedish neutrality by sending submarines into Swedish waters, it is not impossible that the whole Swedish attitude to the Community might be reviewed with the result that Sweden might climb off the fence and join the family of free Europeans.

FINLAND
The foreign relations of Finland are dominated by its huge eastern neighbour, the Soviet Union. For Finland to try to join the European Community at present would be interpreted by the Russians as an

unfriendly act. Joining the Community is therefore not possible for the Finns at present.

AUSTRIA
The Austrians believe thay are forced to remain neutral by the Treaty that gave them their freedom from Soviet occupation in 1955. Otherwise it is probable that they would join the Community as quickly as possible.

SWITZERLAND
Switzerland is a traditionally neutral country. It does not even belong to the United Nations. The very prosperous Swiss feel no need to change their present situation, while being protected by the shadow of N.A.T.O. and having made themselves as difficult for an attacker to swallow as a hedgehog.

THE REAL CHOICE FOR BRITAIN IS NOT ABOUT LEAVING THE COMMUNITY
The real choice which faces the British people today is not about leaving the Community. Leaving is not a real option. The real choice is different. Given that we have to stay as members, the real choice is whether or not we wish to obtain the maximum benefits from our membership by becoming wholehearted members—or whether we prefer to continue, as now, as halfhearted members, dragging our feet and receiving correspondingly fewer benefits. This real choice is discussed in the following chapters. The British people would demand to be more involved in Community affairs if only they realised how many benefits are being denied to them at present.

CHAPTER TWO

The True Choice Now Facing The British People

The choice which now faces the British people is not whether we should stay in the European Community: that is not a real question—because we can not afford to cut ourselves off from its decision making. The true choice is: do we wish to continue as *halfhearted* members of the Community—or should we start to make a wholehearted effort so that we get as much out of the Community as the French do? The real question is: should we make a greater effort in Europe in order to obtain more benefits, rather than merely haggling to reduce our net financial payment to the minimum?

BRITAIN'S POTENTIAL ROLE—AS A LEADER OF EUROPE?
The British dilemma was encapsulated in a famous remark by Dean Acheson, who was the American Secretary of State from 1951 to 1953: "Great Britain has lost an empire but has not yet found a role." It is surely time that we British faced up to the new role that history and geography have given to us—which is to be a part of Europe—and that we enter into the new role with enthusiasm.

Our real choice is not whether we are to be an isolated island people: it is whether or not we should continue to allow our continental neighbours to lead the way with new initiatives while we drag our feet. The hard truth is that there has never yet been a positive new initiative by the British in Europe! Instead of our present negative approach, the British could be setting the lead in the shaping of the new Europe.

If the British people conclude that they should remain in the European Community—in order to share in the decisions and to enjoy the benefits of increasing trade—then what should Britain's role in the Community be?

OUR MISERABLY CAUTIOUS ATTITUDE TO EUROPE SINCE 1945
The cautious approach of the British to initiatives in Europe ever since

1945 has been to watch sceptically from the sidelines to see if an initiative turned into anything lasting. If a continental initiative proved to be successful the British policy would be "pragmatic"—to acknowledge its surprising success, to work with it accordingly, and to try to force through changes in any rules which did not suit us.

Consequently Britain's record since 1945 in respect of new European developments has been totally negative. We have been late in recognising the significance of every single initiative: we always remained initially on the sidelines expressing our doubts, and *we have always joined in later*. It is now widely accepted in Britain that our refusal to join the Common Market at its birth in 1957 was a mistake. By remaining on the sidelines, we allowed the continentals to write the rules of the Common Agricultural Policy to suit themselves. Later, when we were finally able to join in 1973, we discovered that their rules had not been written to suit us. Since then we have spent considerable time and energy arguing for changes without much success.

For the future, the British people ought now to decide that their best prospects lie with participating fully in European developments particularly at their beginnings—and in leading them, rather than standing on the sidelines sceptically.

When in 1957 the French Parliament debated whether or not France should join the proposed new European Economic Community, one of their members, Alain Savary, put his country's choice very starkly: "The choice is not between the Community and the status quo, but between the Community and solitude." It is the same choice now for Britain. The French decided to plunge in wholeheartedly in order to obtain the most benefits out of it: surely we British should be doing the same?

WE SHARE THE SAME PROBLEMS AS THE CONTINENTALS
Every west European nation has suffered a dramatic decline in influence on world affairs during the twentieth century. The nations which all possessed empires at the start of the twentieth century have now lost them—Great Britain, Netherlands, France, Germany, Italy and Austria-Hungary. The now small nations of western Europe have less ability to choose separate destinies for themselves. The two federal super powers, the U.S.A. and the U.S.S.R., now make the major decisions that affect us all.

New technological discoveries brought peoples throughout the world closer together through the development of telephones, television, computers, satellites, and cheap mass travel.

THE GROWING INADEQUACY OF THE NATION STATE CONCEPT
These changes have made the historical concept of "the Nation State" too narrow for it to fully encompass all the interests of its citizens any longer. People increasingly wish to travel, to trade and to live wherever they choose. New technologies do not recognise national boundaries. Ecological disasters do not limit themselves national frontiers. Economic problems such as unemployment, inflation, and recession are common problems faced by all European peoples. Europeans everywhere wish to defend their freedom and their liberties against the expansionist Communism of the U.S.S.R. None of these twentieth century developments can be solved individually by any one of Europe's many nation states.

The nation state is an increasingly inadequate concept for dealing with these problems. In some situations, the developing aspirations of the European peoples are actually hindered by the existence of the nation states. The freedom of the peoples of Europe are diminished by there being different currencies, different frontier regulations, national passport controls and national customs checks.

To the European question "How do we solve our common problems?" the answer surely must be "Through common solutions," rather than through twelve separate national solutions. When a complex international problem has arisen in the past, the traditional approach has been for national politicians, all of goodwill, to come together from their national capitals and to draft an apparently unanimous solution which included as much agreement as possible and which papered over their differences. It was almost impossible for twelve negotiators from different backgrounds to quickly reach a unanimous agreement which was not banal. If their agreement was meaningful, there was no mechanism for enforcing it effectively and fairly through twelve equal partners, none of which had the right to enforce anything on the others. Without provision for supranational enforcement, the agreement could be and would be broken at will by one or by all of the individual nations. The consequence was that the minimal solution was chosen for the peoples of Europe instead of the optimal. Examples are common:

THE LESS THAN PERFECT DEFENCE OF EUROPE

The arrangements for defence in Europe are imperfect because of the separateness of its nation states. Each nation prefers to retain as much control over its own forces as it possibly can; each nation prefers to make its own choice of equipment, spare parts and ammunition types.

During the present decade, all the European nations in N.A.T.O. *except one* agreed to standardise on a particular type of shell for their army tanks. For the British the good news was that the shell was British made: the bad news was that the one nation which chose to be different was Britain because it preferred to continue to use an American made shell!

In order to reduce the mounting costs of our defence, we need longer production runs—which has to mean standardised defence equipment. Not all the free nations of western Europe agree to work for our mutual defence. One European Community nation, the Republic of Ireland, remains neutral partly because of a historical grudge against the British; two other countries, France and Spain are members of N.A.T.O. for planning purposes but insist that only their own generals shall command their own national military forces. Even though Europe is as rich as the U.S.A. our security depends on the American military forces which are stationed in Europe.

It may be that the pressures already visible in the U.S.A., but not yet commanding a majority, will lead to an eventual American withdrawal from Europe. Before very long, Europe may have to organise its own defence including its own nuclear deterrent.

WE ARE EACH TOO SMALL AND TOO SLOW

Each nation state in Europe is now too small to influence world events by itself. Slowly and gradually, a tide of history is pushing the peoples of Europe to recognise that their problems and their interests are similar—and to recognise that by acting together they will have greater success than any of them will have separately. Only by acting together will the European peoples regain their lost power to influence world events and be able to resist external pressures imposed upon them by superpowers, present and future.

But, the present speed of growing together of the European peoples is slow. It cannot be assumed that there will be plenty of time in which to do it. The technological lead held by the Japanese and the Americans over Europe is severe and increasing. The military threat from the ever more strongly armed Soviet Union cannot be overlooked. What exactly do they want those massive weapons for? Time cannot be assumed to be automatically on Europe's side. Halfhearted participation by the nation states in the process of uniting Europe could prove to be too little and too late.

CLOUDS OF HISTORY WITH WHICH WE ALL TRAVEL

It is not easy for nation states with rich histories to co-operate effectively together. It would all be so much simpler if each could forget its past. But all Europeans drag invisible clouds of history behind them. The clouds distort their perception of their present lack of importance and of their feelings about each other.

Each national government is an expression of its own national history. Each national government is reluctant to pool its national inheritance for the greater common good of all European peoples. Their inertia is reinforced because a national government, like every other bureaucratic organisation, is reluctant to surrender any of its powers, however strong the arguments may be for doing so. There is little willingness by our national government to agree that membership of a larger Community is not a zero sum game in which one people must necessarily be losing if another is seen to be gaining. Our national parliament is unwilling to admit that Europe's combined strength is greater than the sum of the strength of its individual nations, because to do so would be to accept an inevitable reduction in its own importance.

OUR TOO SMALL INFLUENCE ON WORLD EVENTS

The influence on world events by Europeans is smaller than it should be. The European Community is a giant industrially but it is still a dwarf politically. Europe is insufficiently organised to be able to exert its proper influence in the world. Our Community is the greatest trading power in the world; it provides more development aid to the Third World than anybody else; the combined population of the Community is greater than the populations of the U.S.A. and of the U.S.S.R.; the combined Gross Domestic Product is equal to the U.S.A. Yet the Community's influence is far less than that of either the Americans or of the Soviet Union.

Most Europeans believe that the turbulent state of world affairs would benefit from a stronger influence from Europe. But Europeans will only achieve that influence by unifying their own voices. Only by unifying—rather than through a compromise among twelve proud Foreign Secretaries—will Europeans effectively meet the challenge of world events.

EUROPE'S UNCOORDINATED INDUSTRIAL STRENGTH
Political strength comes from economic strength. Economic strength comes from having a large home market. To be able to compete with the economic giants such as the U.S.A. and Japan, Europe's small nations need to pool their individual markets. Both the U.S.A. and Japan have larger homogeneous home markets each involving only a single language: in addition Japan's is protected by strong non-tariff barriers against imports. Elsewhere, but so far undeveloped, China has over one thousand million people, India six hundred million, and Indonesia an hundred and thirty million, all potentially able to dwarf us.

The American home market contains over two hundred million consumers, and the Japanese market has over a hundred million. Against this, the largest national market in Europe is West Germany with a population of only sixty million people.

Very worryingly we are becoming net importers of telecommunications equipment although the Community still has an overall trade surplus in high technology. The balance of payments is moving against Europeans in the new technologies which will provide the jobs of the future.

This is because European businesses cannot achieve sufficient economies of scale. This problem was part of the original thinking that led to the setting up of the Common Market in 1957. However there still is no real common market in Europe, because the national governments refuse to give up their frontier controls and their rights to decide industrial standards inside their own state. A wholehearted effort by the British to lead Europe towards true industrial and political strength would be inestimably worthwhile to ourselves and to all Europeans. At present we call loudly for a true common market but we allow all the other countries to secretly veto our proposals if they like.

OUR REAL CHOICE
The previous President of Greece, Mr. Karamanlis, put the real choice for all Europeans very clearly in his speech to the European Parliament at Strasbourg in Sepetember 1983. He said that we have to choose

whether or not we allow Europe to revert to its original role as *an appendage of Asia*. His exact words were:

"I cannot but remind you all of our historic responsibilities. And faced with the uncertainty of our options, I wonder: will Europe become what it is in reality, a small appendage of the Asian continent? Or will it remain what it appears to be, that is the precious part of the universe, the pearl of the earth, the brain of the body?"

The idea of European unity has been called 'the greatest idea of the twentieth century'. On its success or failure rest the prospects of future generations of Europeans. The question now for the British people is whether they wish to fully participate and even to lead in the process of strengthening Europe—or whether they prefer to continue to do things their own way, to drag their feet in connection with Europe and so to allow the French and the Germans to decide what happens to us all.

The British people are uncertain about this choice because they can see few direct benefits so far from having joined the Community. The reason for this disappointment—which is easily identifiable but is kept secret from the public—will be examined in Chapter Four. But to make Britain's predicament clear, it is helpful to follow quickly in the footsteps towards unity that Europeans have been taking ever since the end of the Second European Civil War in 1945.

CHAPTER THREE

The March to European Unity Since 1946

Guaranteed and unrestricted access into the market of France, Germany and elsewhere on the continent is essential for us if we are to continue to earn our keep in the world. But these are no longer separate national markets. The barriers between the continental markets have been eroding for nearly thirty years as a result of a continuous and intentional march towards the unification of Europe.

This march towards unity among the separate nations of Western Europe arose as a direct consequence of the disaster of the Second World War. The Second World War was also a Second European Civil War from which the only real victors have proved to be non-Europeans, in particular the U.S.A. and the U.S.S.R. All the European nations were seriously weakened by their efforts to destroy each other twice during this century.

PRE-ECHOES

Even before 1939, there had been pre-echoes of the idea of European unity. The concept of a "United States of Europe" was first mentioned by Victor Hugo in the middle of the nineteenth century. It was discussed during the 1920s and 1930s by such political thinkers as Stresemann of Germany, Briand of France and by the out-of-power Winston Churchill. But nothing concrete developed from their discussions.

The first attempted step towards unity was made in June 1940 when Churchill offered the French full political union between the United Kingdom and France. But his offer failed because it was overtaken on the same day when the beleagured French government, believing that France could no longer defend herself, appointed Petain to negotiate for peace with the Nazis.

However Churchill, remarkably considering what year it was,

continued to think ahead and wrote privately in 1942 to Sir Anthony Eden that:

"I must admit that my thoughts rest primarily in Europe . . . It would be a measureless disaster if Russian barbarism over laid the culture and independence of the ancient states of Europe . . . Hard as it is to say now, I trust that the European family may act unitedly as one . . . I look forward to a United States of Europe . . . I hope to see the economy of Europe studied as a whole . . . Of course we shall have to work with the Americans in many ways, and in the greatest ways, but Europe is our prime care . . ."

FIRST SPARK OF ACTION

The first spark of European unification was lit by Winston Churchill through his speech at Zurich University on 19th September, 1946, a speech that has become immortal. He entitled it "A Call to the Youth of the World". In it he called publicly for the creation of "a kind of United States of Europe". He carefully did not say whether or not he believed the United Kingdom should join the United States of Europe. But in the four decades since Churchill made the speech, Britain's relative importance in the world has declined dramatically. If in 1946 he envisaged us remaining apart from a federal Europe and continuing to trade with our British Empire, it seems likely today that we would be advised to join with the other European peoples, the sun having set with certainty on the British Empire.

Forty years later, Churchill's words at Zurich still repay being read in full. He said:

"We all know that the two world wars through which we have passed arose out of the vain passion of a newly united Germany to play the dominating part in the world. In this last struggle, crimes and massacres have been committed for which there is no parallel since the invasion of the Mongols in the fourteenth century, and no equal at any time in human history. The guilty must be punished. Germany must be deprived of the power to re-arm and make another aggressive war.

But when all this has been done, as it will be done, as it is being done, then there must be an end to retribution. There must be what Mr. Gladstone many years ago called a Blessed Act of Oblivion. We must all turn our backs upon the horrors of the past. We must look to the future. We cannot afford to drag forward across the years that are to come, the hatreds and revenges which have sprung from the injuries of the past. If Europe is to be saved from infinite misery and indeed from final doom, there must be this act of faith in the European family and this act of oblivion against all the crimes and follies of the past.

Can the free peoples of Europe rise to the height of these resolves of the soul and of the instincts of the spirit of man? If they can, the wrongs and injuries which have been inflicted will have been washed away on all sides by the miseries which have been endured. Is there any need for further floods of agony? Is the only lesson of history to be that mankind is unteachable? Let there be justice, mercy and freedom. The people have only to will it, and all will achieve their heart's desire. I am now going to say something that will astonish you.

The first step in the recreation of the European family must be a partnership between France and Germany. In this way only can France recover the moral and cultural leadership of Europe. There can be no revival of Europe without a spiritually great France and a spiritually great Germany.

The structure of the United States of Europe, if well and truly built, will be such as to make the material strength of a single state less important. Small nations will count as much as large ones and gain their honour by their contribution to the common cause. The ancient states and principalities of Germany, freely together for mutual convenience in a federal system, might take their individual places among the United States of Europe.

I shall not try to make a detailed programme for hundreds of millions of people who want to be happy and free, prosperous and safe, who wish to enjoy the four freedoms of which the great President Roosevelt spoke, and live in accordance with the principles embodied in the Atlantic Charter. If this is their wish, if this is the wish of Europeans in so many lands, they have only to say so, and means can certainly be found and machinery erected to carry that wish to full fruition.

But I must give you a warning. Time may be short. At present there is a breathing space. The cannons have ceased firing. The fighting has stopped. But the dangers have not stopped. If we are to form a United States of Europe, or whatever name it may take, we must begin now.

In these present days we dwell strangely and precariously under the shield, and I will even say protection, of the atomic bomb. The atomic bomb is still only in the hands of a state and nation which we know will never use it except in the cause of right and freedom. But it may well be that in a few years this awful agency of destruction will be widespread. And the catastrophe following from its use by several warring nations will not only bring to an end all that we call civilisation, but may possibly disintegrate the globe itself.

I must now sum up the propositions which are before you. Our constant aim must be to build and fortify the strength of the United Nations Organisation. Under and within that world concept we must re-create the European family in a regional structure—called it may be the United States of Europe. And the first practical step would be to form a Council of Europe. If at first, all the States of Europe are not willing, or able, to join the Union, we must nevertheless proceed to assemble and combine those who will and those who can.

The salvation of the common people of every race and of every land from war or servitude must be established on solid foundations, and must be guarded by the readiness of all men and women to die rather than submit to tyranny. In all this urgent work France and Germany must take the lead together. Great Britain, the British Commonwealth of Nations, mighty America and, I trust, Soviet Russia for then indeed all would be well, must be the friends and sponsors of the new Europe, and must champion its right to live and shine.

Therefore I say to you: 'Let Europe arise'."

Winston Churchill was out of power in Britain in 1946. But even the current British Foreign Secretary, Labour's Ernest Bevin, shared the mood for having fewer national barriers. Bevin said: "Diplomats asked me in London what the aim of my foreign policy really was. And I said, to go down to Victoria Station, get a railway ticket and go where the hell I liked without a passport or anything else."

FIRST, THE O.E.C.C. AND THE COUNCIL OF EUROPE

Even though Churchill was out of power, his words led to the formation of the Organisation for European Economic Co-operation (the

O.E.C.C. now called the O.E.C.D.) for co-ordinating receipt of Marshall Plan aid from the U.S.A. Churchill's proposal to have a Council of Europe was acted upon at Strasbourg on the Franco-German border in 1949: it still exists as a useful debating society without powers. It is composed of members sent from the national parliaments of twenty-one democratic European countries. It produced the very valuable European Convention of Human Rights based on the United Nations' earlier Universal Declaration of Human Rights. The European Convention has been made enforceable in law by most European countries: disputes are resolved by a decision of the European Court of Human Rights at Strasbourg.

NEXT, COAL AND STEEL UNION

On 9th May, 1950 the French Foreign Minister, Robert Schuman, proposed another new idea—the placing under *international control* of coal and steel production in Europe. This idea, fathered by a visionary French civil servant, Jean Monnet, was revolutionary. It would voluntarily transfer control of weapon-making industries, coal and steel, out of the hands of national governments and into the hands of a supranational body for the first time in all history. In Schuman's own words: "By the pooling of basic production and the establishment of a new High Authority whose decisions will be binding on France, Germany and the countries that join them, this proposal will lay the first concrete foundations of the European Federation which is indispensable to the maintenance of peace." Jean Monnet said: "We are undertaking a common task—not to negotiate for our own advantage but to seek it in the advantage of all."

France, Germany, Italy and the three small Benelux countries (Belgium, Netherlands and Luxembourg) accepted the idea. The Treaty of Paris was signed in 1951 which set up the European Coal and Steel Community for fifty years. The United Kingdom government did not take part.

THEN, A EUROPEAN ARMY?

Speaking at the Council of Europe at Strasbourg in 1950, Churchill had proposed the idea of a single European Army unified command with soldiers from different countries in identical uniforms. The developing Cold War in Europe and the communist invasion of South Korea strengthened the idea. A draft treaty was actually initialled in 1952 to form a European Defence Community. The German parliament ratified it in 1953, but keen controversy continued. The British government rejected the whole idea. The idea finally died when the French parliament refused to ratify the treaty because of a change in their government and because of France's needs to use its own forces for its war in Indo-China. Instead the six Coal and Steel Community countries plus Britain created a "Western European Union" as a debating society in which Europe's defence could be discussed.

MONNET'S ACTION COMMITTEE
New ideas for unification in Europe continued to appear. In 1955, Jean Monnet set up his unofficial "Action Committee for the United States of Europe". This was to become a famous source and driving force for new ideas and initiatives. Subsequently, in 1968, *all* three major British political parties joined his Committee although, regrettably, none boasts about it today.

CONFERENCE AT MESSINA
The failure to set up a European Defence community was a major setback. To revive momentum towards European unification, the Foreign Ministers of the same Six countries of the Coal and Steel Community met at Messina in Italy in June 1955. The British refused to participate and did not even send an observer. The Six agreed to continue their attempts to unite Europe. They appointed Paul-Henri Spaak, then Belgian Foreign Minister, to prepare a report on economic union.

Just less than a year later, the Six met again at a follow-up conference in Venice. They accepted Spaak's proposals that they co-operate in nuclear energy and that they create "a common market".

COMMON MARKET AND EURATOM
Formal negotiations between the Six immediately started. The Treaty of Rome was signed on 25th March, 1957 creating the European Economic Community (known also as the Common Market) which came into effect on 1st January, 1958. Its objective was free movement for goods, persons, services and capital by abolishing all trade barriers between the six signatory countries. The British, under Prime Minister Eden, decided not to take part.

In nuclear energy the Germans were doubtful about Spaak's recommendation of co-operation because it might threaten their own expanding nuclear industry. The French were suspicious of the Germans because they believed their own nuclear industry was weak and needed protection. Nevertheless an annex to the Rome Treaty was signed by the same Six states the following month to create the European Atomic Energy Community (now known as Euratom). Its purpose was to foster joint progress in the peaceful uses of nuclear energy. The British did not take part.

EUROPEAN FREE TRADE AREA

The British instead announced their preference for a free trade area which would have no supanational controls. We attempted unsuccessfully to persuade the Six to abandon their new political commitment to each other and to join us in creating a free trade area embracing all of Europe. So we gathered six of the remaining small nations of Europe together to form the European Free Trade Area, (known as E.F.T.A.) which was inaugurated in May 1960. It consisted of Austria, Denmark, Norway, Portugal, Sweden, Switzerland and ourselves. Finland became an associated member in 1961. Iceland joined in 1970.

WE THEN CHANGE OUR MIND AND PREFER THE COMMUNITY

Only one summer later in 1961, Prime Minister Harold Macmillan reversed British policy and applied for Britain to join all the Communities (Coal and Steel, Common Market, and Euratom). Denmark and Ireland immediately followed our example, and Norway applied the following year. Greece, Turkey, Spain and Portugal asked for associated status with the Community.

However, in January 1963 General de Gaulle, then President of France, vetoed the British application to join. Negotiations between the E.E.C. and the four applicant countries had to be indefinitely suspended.

In 1967, under Harold Wilson's premiership, the British government re-applied to join but General de Gaulle remained as opposed as ever. Only after he resigned from the French Presidency in the summer of 1969 could negotiations be resumed.

Negotiations were successful this time. In January 1972, Treaties of

Accession were signed between original the Six member states and the four new countries. But only nine out of the ten national parliaments ratified them. The exception was Norway, where a referendum narrowly rejected its government's proposal to join the Community. So only the United Kingdom, the Republic of Ireland and Denmark joined the European Communities in January 1973.

Greece joined in 1981 to make ten member countries. Portugal and Spain became the eleventh and twelfth members in January 1986.

OTHER STEPS TOWARDS UNITY

Alongside these political steps towards unity, integration also started in other fields.

In sport, soccer ceased to have purely national competitions: European-wide competitions were initiated. However, sharing the same suspicions as Britain's national politicians, the English soccer authorities would not allow their champion club, Chelsea, to take part in the first European-wide contest. Now, a quarter of a century later, it is the chief ambition of every British football club to qualify to play in a European competition.

The first cuts in customs duties between the Six member states inside the Community were made in January 1959. Progressively, further cuts were made until all duties were eliminated in July 1968. A uniform external customs tariff was also agreed for trade between the Six member states and the rest of the world.

The Social Fund was initiated in 1960 to help train people to adapt to the changing economic situation. Since then, the Fund has grown considerably at the insistance of the European Parliament.

The first regulation to give workers the right of free movement came into effect in 1961. It has led to the right which we all have, of being free to work wherever we choose within the Community.

The world's broadest ever trade agreement was signed at Yaounde in Africa in 1963 between the Six and seventeen African nations. Its purpose was to assist the exports of developing countries. Subsequently many other developing states have joined. A total now of sixty-four from Africa, the Pacific and the Caribbean are associated with the European Community through a treaty now called the Lomé Convention. It provides that 99.5 per cent of the Lomé countries' exports may enter the Community markets tariff-free, but allows the Lomé countries to put up tariffs against Community exports to them. It also guarantees that the Community will import sugar from the Caribbean despite being able to produce more than enough itself and guarantees that it will pay the European price for it which is above the world price.

In January 1963 a Franco-German Friendship Treaty was signed. This was particularly significant for the future goal of a united Europe because it met the original objective of the Community—of abolishing war between the two countries who had fought each other three times in ninety years.

Rules for the Common Agriculture Policy were agreed in 1964 after long and sometimes bitter negotiations between the original Six members. Britain had excluded herself from the debate by having refused to join the Community in 1957: we still suffer today from our failure to join originally so that we could take an active role in deciding the rules about agriculture.

In 1965 there were proposals for giving the Community its own financial resources and for strengthening the European Parliament. They were resisted by De Gaulle, but they were accepted in 1970 after his death.

The Regional Fund was commenced in 1975, with the objective of assisting the less developed regions of the Community. It is not clear whether this policy has been successful, particularly since it is believed that the governments of certain member states of the Community merely pocket the money from Brussels and do not spend it in the regions as they have agreed to do.

The European Monetary System (E.M.S.) came into operation in 1979. It has four objectives—a mechanism to stabilise the members states' currencies within pre-agreed limits; credit facilities; transfer arrangements; and the European Currency Unit (the "E.C.U."). The British government has never played a full part in the E.M.S., being sceptical and preferring to watch on the sidelines.

Contrary to British scepticism, the E.M.S. has proved to be a great success. It has established an area of exchange rate stability for the continental currencies. The British government's attitude has now changed to "We will join but the time is not yet right". When the world's speculators drove the pound sterling down in early 1985 they were able to do so because they knew it did not have to be defended by the other E.E.C. central banks. Had we already been full members at that time, British traders would have benefitted.

In June 1979 the European Parliament was directly elected for the first time by the peoples of the Community, the first ever international parliament. Previous to 1979 there had been a smaller European Parliament but its members were appointed by national governments and so were under their direct control. The new directly-elected Members of the European Parliament (called M.E.P.s or Euro—M.P.s) are independent of control by national governments—and are therefore able to concentrate on furthering the development of European unification, free from national blinkers.

A Common Fisheries Policy was finally agreed after long negotiations between the ten member states of the Community in 1983. Contrary to popular opinion, it did not destroy the British fishing fleet. Our fishermens' problems stemmed from the unilateral declaration by Iceland of a two hundred mile limit around its own coast. Unfortunately the backward-looking reaction of the British government was to send gunboats! The consequence is that British fishing vessels are now excluded from the rich Icelandic fishing grounds while vessels from other Community states are allowed to fish there.

The Community's own centre for thermonuclear fusion research, the Joint European Torus (known as J.E.T.), became operational at Culham in Oxfordshire in 1983. It is now too expensive for such large-scale research projects to be undertaken by a single European country on its own. In this case the cost are shared by the Community countries plus Switzerland and Sweden.

The European Strategic Programme of Research in Information Technology (known as E.S.P.R.I.T.) was launched by the Community in 1984. If Europeans are ever to be able to catch up with the Japanese and the Americans in the new sunrise industries (such as Information Technology and Fifth Generation Computers) we have to co-operate together. There is no value in each European country financing its own separate research in these areas because we shall each cover the same initial ground. None of us has the resources of the Americans or of the Japanese. None of us individually can get ahead of them. But Europeans working together may be able to do so. Sadly, due to petty vetoes from certain national ministers in the Council of Ministers, this common programme took two years to be agreed, during which time Europe fell further behind its competitors.

Joint development of a plutonium fast breeder reactor was agreed by six of the Community states including Britain in 1984.

OTHER EUROPEAN PROJECTS

There are also a number of European projects which are not financed by all the Community states. But their existence convincingly demonstrates the huge benefits of working together in the face of American and Japanese competition.

A particle physics laboratory for Europe, C.E.R.N. (in full, "Conseil Europeen pour la Recherche Nucleaire") was founded in 1954. Situated on both sides of the Franco-Swiss border near Geneva, it is financed by thirteen European states among which are eight members of the Community including Britain. Its considerable success has caused one leading American professor to call it "a symbol of the United States of Europe."

For space research, the European rocket-launcher "Ariane" has proved very successful as a competitor to the American space shuttle. Sadly for the British we contribute only a two per cent interest: the French have the major share.

In military aircraft construction, the "Tornado" was built by a joint Italian-German-British company.

In commercial aircraft construction, the European Airbus Consortium has competed with increasing success against the well established American plane makers. Sadly, again, the now-privatised British interest is only twenty per cent.

These footsteps over the past forty years—all consistent with the theme of uniting the peoples of Europe—are part of a continuing process. Now the choice facing the British people is this: can we afford to go on dragging our feet? Can we afford to ignore the next steps? Can we even afford to continue to treat them halfheartedly?

CHAPTER FOUR

But Where Are Our Benefits So Far?

The British man or woman in the street remains doubtful abour our membership of the Community. Usually their question is: "Where are the benefits we were promised from Britain's membership?" To many people there appear to have been few benefits, if any, from our joining: to some people it appears that there have only been disadvantages. Opinion polls show a substantial proportion of the British public to be still *against* our membership of the European Community—even though paradoxically to the usual next question a substantial proportion of them then declares themselves in *favour* of more European unification.

Those who—like the author—advocate further integration of the British people into Europe must explain why those benefits have not yet arrived, and must give hope that they will arrive, preferably soon.

HIGH EXPECTATIONS, LOW RESULTS

Joining the European Community in 1973 gave the British people many and different expectations: some longed for enduring peace in Europe, others looked forward to cheaper wine and motorcars, others to abolishing passports and other barriers to free movement, others that their professional qualifications would be recognised in all Community countries. Few of their expectations, apart from enduring peace, have yet been realised.

Business and industry in Britain expected that there would be fewer barriers to imports and exports. Although there are now no formal tariffs inside the Community, there is still an abundance of hidden non-tariff barriers put up by every national government (including our own) in order to hinder imports from other Community states. The promised harmonisation of trading standards and abolition of non-tariff barriers between member states has proceeded at only a snail's pace.

Why has so little been achieved? What has gone wrong? Whose fault is it? The answer to these questions are a mystery to the British public. They may even be a mystery to some backbenchers in the House of Commons. There certainly never has been a debate within any political party in Britain to discover why the European Community is not working properly, and how it could be improved. Nevertheless, British government ministers and their senior civil servants who negotiate in Brussels on behalf of the British people, know exactly why the Community has not produced the promised benefits. And the answer to the mystery is surprisingly simple.

HOW THE COMMUNITY WORKS
At this point it is necessary to explain briefly how the Community works. The Community has four principal institutions. They are entirely distinct from each other in order to observe a basic principle of democracy, the separation of powers. The four separate institutions are: the Commission (which is the civil service), the Council of Ministers, the European Parliament and the European Court of Justice. Their responsibilities which are set out in the Treaty of Rome are:
1. the Commission has the sole responsibility for proposing legislation and for day by day administration of the Community;
2. the Council of Ministers has the task of making the final decision about the Commission's proposals, whether to accept or reject them;
3. the Parliament has the job of ensuring democratic acceptability of the Commission's and Council's actions;
4. the Court of Justice adjudicates in disputes.

WHICH OF THE FOUR INSTITUTIONS IS TO BLAME FOR THE ABSENCE OF BENEFITS?
The lack of benefits for the public is not the fault of Europe's civil servants in the Commission: they have proposed the necessary draft legislation. Often accused of being a bloated bureaucracy living in ivory towers in Brussels, the Commission is small and effective. It employs only about twenty thousand people—about the same number as a British county council—of whom one third do the unavoidable work of language translation: the Community's civil service is tiny compared with the half million civil servants whom the public have to pay taxes for in Britain.

Nor is the lack of benefits because of any failure of the European

Parliament or of the Court of Justice; both have stayed up-to-date with their responsibilities.

THE BLAME LIES SQUARELY WITH THE COUNCIL OF MINISTERS
The blame for the Community's failures lies almost entirely with the national governments of the member states! This was admitted by the Irish Prime Minister, Dr. Garret FitzGerald, in his speech to the European Parliament on 25th July, 1984. His exact words were:

"Let me at this stage say, without exonerating any of our European institutions, that the primary responsibility for most of these failures falls on Member States governments, in the manner in which we as governments have conducted ourselves in the Council of Ministers in its various forms. There is, indeed, it seems to me, a certain injustice in the fact that as governments we have escaped some of our share of the blame for the deficiencies of our Community, and that a disproportionate share of that blame has been visited by our people upon the European Parliament."

UNOFFICIAL SECRET VETOES BY NATIONAL MINISTERS
The failure to which Dr. FitzGerald referred is the unwillingness of the national governments to take *small-scale* decisions which would improve the working of the Community. Instead of taking decisions, the national governments allow each other to have an automatic right of veto over any proposal which any *one* of them dislikes! Consequently, many of the Community's proposals for improvements and benefits are vetoed, even though they would introduce benefits to the public.

Currently over four hundred different Commission proposals are blocked by a national veto from one or other government in the Council of Ministers! Until 1985, the oldest vetoed proposal, dating from 1967, was a proposal that architects' qualifications should be mutually recognised in all member states; in other words a British qualified architect should be able to practice on the continent, a French architect in Britain, and so on. This proposal was secretly vetoed without explanation by Germany ever since 1967 and the other national governments raised no serious objection to the secret German veto!

A matter which is vetoed by certain national ministers is a single seat for the European Parliament. The Treaty of Rome states that the European Parliament shall have a single working place, but unfortunately it gives the Council of Ministers the right to decide where that will be. Taxpayers are penalised by an extra twenty million pounds per year to move the Parliament's files and officials around Europe. The European Parliament receives public scorn for its apparent indecision about where to meet—while national ministers escape scotfree from the blame. Even the British government, when asked to help by British M.E.P.s, has been unwilling to publicly back the Parliament in its search to improve public economy and its own efficiency.

The huge butter mountain is a scandal caused by the vetoes of national ministers. The European Parliament drew attention to the growing surplus of butter as long ago as 1981. It pointed out that public consumption of dairy products was falling while milk production by farmers was rising. The Parliament asked the Council of Ministers to take corrective action in good time. However the national ministers could never find a good time to take the painful decision to control the dairy farmers: there was always a national election coming up somewhere which meant there was always a national minister who felt obliged to veto the proposal to cutback milk production. The Council of Agriculture Ministers only took a decision to impose quotas on dairy farmers in the spring of 1984 at very short notice: it only did so because there was no money left in the E.E.C. Budget to allow them to finance a further delay by having an even bigger butter mountain. Up to that moment, the British government was actively encouraging British dairy farmers to *expand* their milk production!

THESE VETOES HAVE NO LEGAL BASIS

What is astonishing is that most of the vetoes in the Council of Ministers are unofficial: most of the vetoes have no legal basis in the Treaty of Rome. This is carefully concealed from the public by national ministers: otherwise, the public might ask them whether *vetoes obstruct benefits*.

NATIONAL MINISTERS SHOULD BE FORCED TO "VOTE NOT VETO"

How has this extraordinary situation come about? The national ministers are required by the Treaty of Rome to take decisions together in the Council of Ministers through *voting by majority*. The rules about having to vote are set out clearly in the Treaty of Rome and were accepted by every country without amendment when they each first joined.

To prevent there being narrowly contested votes which might lead to bitterness, a minimum majority of around two-thirds in favour is required before a proposal can be passed. The rules give the large countries more votes than the smaller ones, as follows:

Belgium	5	Italy	10
Denmark	3	Luxembourg	2
Germany	10	Netherlands	5
Greece	5	Portugal	5
France	10	Spain	8
Ireland	3	United Kingdom	10

It takes only a minority to reject a Community proposal. This is deliberate so that a large state like the United Kingdom with ten votes should rarely be outvoted.

GENUINE VETOES ARE ALLOWED IN CERTAIN DEFINED SITUATIONS
A genuine Veto is allowed in about thirty-two major situations. These are specifically defined in the Treaty of Rome. In these cases, all members of the Council of Ministers must agree together unanimously before a proposal can be passed.

The following is a list of the most important situations when each national minister has a genuine veto. The figures in brackets are the number of the relevant Article in the Treaty of Rome:

	Article No:
Permanent changes in customs duties	(28)
Social security for migrant workers	(51)
Freedom of establishment for non-member state nationals	(59)
Free movement of capital	(70)
Certain derogations from common transport policy	(75.3)
Sea and Air transport policy	(85)
Certain derogations permitting state aids	(93)
Harmonisation of indirect taxes	(99)
Measures affecting the direct functioning of the Common Market	(100)
Conjunctural economic policies	(103)
Delegated powers to the Commission on social security matters	(121)
New activities for the Social Fund	(126)

Elections to the European Parliament (138)
Amendments to Commission proposals (149)
Increasing the numbers of Judges (165)
Increasing the Community's own financial resources (201)
Financial Regulations (209)
Lists of strategic materials exempted from Treaty provisions (223)
Measures to carry objectives of the Treaty into effect (235)
Admission of new member states into the Community (237)
Agreements with non-member countries (238)

On matters of major importance such as these, each and every national government has a genuine veto. But on the less vital topics, the ministers are supposed to vote so that smallscale benefits shall reach the public.

WHY DO NATIONAL MINISTERS PREFER PARALYSING VETOES INSTEAD OF MAKING DECISIONS?

Why then do national ministers fail to take the routine decisions which would bring the public their expected benefits? These unofficial vetoes continue to exist because they are very convenient to national ministers—and because they are kept secret from the public. The Council of Ministers meets in secret: the public and press are never permitted to attend their meetings. Afterwards the ministers announce their decisions, (or their failure by "having stood firm") in their national parliaments. But only rarely do national ministers give the full reasons for their failure to make decisions. The public is kept in blissful ignorance that unexplained and unofficial vetoes cast or permitted by their national rulers have prevented the arrival of benefits which they patiently expect.

Why do national ministers behave like this? Put most simply, it is because national ministers are *afraid* of losing a vote in the Council of Ministers. They fear public criticism from *sectional* interests in their own country. And they fear the loss of their ministerial job. Since by definition, a Community proposal requires a change in current arrangements somewhere, it is predictable that at least one national minister from among all the member states will feel opposed to the proposed change and be therefore at risk of losing the vote. Under the present arrangements for secrecy, any national minister is able to veto any proposal! If he does so, he cannot lose. The other ministers will not outvote him, otherwise they will be outvoted on another occasion. Nobody knows. The public is not told and therefore does not complain. Most national ministers prefer secret indecision to the alternative of their losing a vote publicly, even though a big country like Britain can only lose when in a small minority on a minor issue. They prefer to claim that they are usually defending "national interests" when in truth they are defending sectional interests.

Senior national ministers become anxious about their ability not to lose European decisions, so they increasingly pass responsibility upwards to their own head of government or downwards to their juniors. But the national leaders meet together for two days only three times per year, and they cannot possibly master all the necessary details to take the postponed decisions. Nothing is decided—but the public does not know and does not complain.

Junior ministers also hesitate about taking controversial decisions because their careers might be at risk. They in turn prefer to leave the arguments to their civil servants. But civil servants are not entitled to make decisions, only to discuss them. Consequently, very little is ever decided in the Council of Ministers. But nobody worries—because *the public does not know.*

HOW THE ABUSE STARTED

The abuse started in June 1965. The President of France, General De Gaulle, was unwilling to accept various Community proposals of which the other five states approved. Agreement was not reached within the time set aside in the Council of Ministers. But, instead of agreeing to the usual procedure at that time of "stopping the clock" to allow more time for negotiations the French closed the meeting. De Gaulle withdrew all French government involvement for an indefinite period as a protest: this became known as his "empty chair" policy.

However, the pro-European vote in the French Presidential election of December 1965, forced de Gaulle into a second run-off ballot. In January 1966 De Gaulle agreed sent his Foreign Minister, Couve de Murville, to meetings at Luxembourg with the other five member countries, who had not felt able to continue the development of the European Community without France. At Luxembourg, the six countries *failed* to agree how to solve the problem. The French representatives agreed to resume French participation in the day-to-day working of the Community but insisted that France could not be outvoted "where very important interests are at stake". The other five countries did not agree that the French had any such right. The five jointly stated that "where . . . very important interests of one or more partners are at stake, the members of the Council will endeavour, within a reasonable time, to reach solutions which can be adopted by all."

THERE NEVER WAS A LUXEMBOURG COMPROMISE
A communique which contained *both* these opposing statements was issued at the end of the meeting. It has become known as "the Luxembourg Compromise". But there was *no compromise at Luxembourg*: there was only disagreement. Inevitably, no change was made to the Treaty of Rome, and therefore the French demand to have a unilateral veto has never had a legal basis.

It is said that a junior Luxembourg diplomat was able to ask De Gaulle informally later that year how often he would expect to use a unilateral right of veto. De Gaulle is said to have replied that he expected to use his veto "two or three times in a bad year for France." Yet today over four hundred proposals from the Commission lie vetoed in the Council of Ministers, many of them indisputably not of vital national importance for any member state. But the public is not told.

Today, because the Council of Ministers meets in secret, national ministers do not even have to attempt to justify their vetoes. No thought is given to whether a decision by a majority vote would benefit the public. National civil servants, standing in for their ministers at the Council in Brussels, cast secret vetoes. They block further progress on every proposal if they believe that a sectional interest in their own country would not wish this proposal to go any further, regardless of whether or not the public as a whole would benefit.

A SCANDALOUS ABUSE KEPT SECRETS FROM THE PUBLIC
This is a major scandal. It is totally unknown to the public, both in Britain and throughout the European Community. If the public knew and understood what really happens in the Council of Ministers, and why so many of their expected benefits have not arrived, they ought to be extremely angry. The public should insist that their elected representatives in the Council of Ministers must meet in public and must decide the many overdue but minor decisions by majority voting.

But unless they read this chapter, the public is unlikely to find out!

SECRET VETOES KEEP UNEMPLOYMENT HIGHER THAN NECESSARY
Many of these blocked smaller-scale proposals would lead to *more trade* within the European Community. More free trade would lead to *more jobs* and therefore to *lower unemployment*.

A calculation by the Commission in Brussels indicates that the total cost of getting goods through the Community's internal frontiers is around six and three quarter billion pounds per year. That equals between five and ten per cent of the actual pre-tax value of the goods that is being wasted. The total time wasted by lorries waiting in queues at internal frontiers costs about five hundred million pounds per year. Many extra jobs could be created if those sums were used for investment instead of satisfying national bureaucrats. National governments insist that they need to keep passport and customs controls at their frontiers. Yet, a passport is a nuisance to an honest man and is no deterrent to a dishonest one.

So, by unjustifiably blocking hundreds of routine minor Community decisions in order to protect themselves from criticism by sectional interests in their own countries, national ministers in all national governments are deliberately keeping unemployment higher than it need otherwise be.

The European Parliament recognised that unemployment is a problem common to every Community country. Based on a proposal from a British Conservative M.E.P. Sir Fred Catherwood, it published a plan in 1984 that involved co-ordination of the economic policies of the ten national governments of the Community, so that they would work together to reduce unemployment. But, as usual, the national governments would not agree to act together—and so no action was taken.

National ministers in all ten capitals are deceiving their own peoples, are denying their hopes, are restricting their freedoms, and are lowering their prosperity. The public of Europe is being deceived because national politicians wish to protect sectional interests and their own careers at the public's expense.

ALL NATIONAL GOVERNMENTS SHARE THE GUILT
All national governments in the European Community are guilty of the conspiracy of secret illegal vetoes—either through casting a

veto themselves or by silently permitting others to cast theirs on proposals of which they themselves would have approved. Here are a few examples:

BELGIUM'S
government blocked reform of the Regional Fund because it feared it would lose small grants.

ITALY'S
government caused the failure to move the second stage of the E.M.S., vetoed steel negotiations, and blocked agreement on the milk quotas.

GERMANY'S
government blocked freedom of the insurance market, recognition of architects' qualifications, and proposals to give the E.C.U. full currency status because it would rival the strength of the Deutsch Mark. It also vetoed a small reduction in the support price for cereal growers in 1985 despite the existence of huge grain surpluses.

GREECE'S
government blocked a joint Community condemnation of the shooting down of the Korean airliner by the Soviet Union.

DENMARK'S
government blocks any Community progress in education. It also blocked agreement on the Common Fisheries Policy because it wanted an over large share of the catch so as to grind the extra into fishmeal for fertilisers.

FRANCE'S
government blocked measures to strengthen the internal common market and delayed the admission of Portugal and Spain.

IRELAND'S
government has opposed overdue reforms in agriculture which would reduce unwanted overproduction of food.

LUXEMBOURG'S
government blocks the decision which would give one working place to the European Parliament.

THE UNITED KINGDOM'S
government blocks a uniform proportional voting system for European elections, because it fears that Proportional Representation would prove to be a foot in the door for its national elections even though it already operates proportional representation in Northern Ireland.

Impressively, the Netherlands appear to be the one exception to this catalogue of bad behaviour: it has always believed in the majority vote rule.

LONGTERM NEGATIVE CONSEQUENCES OF THESE SECRET VETOES
If the secret veto which has no legal basis for minor proposals, continues to be used by almost every government, the long term consequence will be paralysis of the Community. The secret veto is good for national politicians in the short-term: but, in the long run, we shall all lose as the bickering little nations of Europe become increasingly overtaken and dominated by the world's economic and military superpowers.

THE LESSON OF HISTORY ABOUT VETOES
History contains many examples of organisations that failed because they gave a right of veto to each of their individual members. The pre-war League of Nations, and the present day Security Council of the United Nations, are tragic examples of well-meaning institutions which are powerless because some of their members have been able to cast an individual veto against any kind of action. The Soviet Union is notorious for its frequent veto to prevent action by the Security Council of the United Nations. At the League of Nations, it was individual vetoes that blocked efforts to find solutions to the invasions of other countries mounted by Japan, Italy and Germany. Because no concerted action was possible to stop these aggressors, the consequence was a second world war.

The Organisation for European Economic Co-operation (now called the O.E.C.D.) was set up by sixteen nations in 1948 to implement a programme for the economic recovery of Europe. However its constitution stated that decisions "shall be taken by mutual agreement of all the countries": in other words decisions had to be unanimous. Today its task is the collection of statistics.

INCONSISTENCY OF THE BRITISH GOVERNMENT'S ATTITUDE
It is absurd for the British government to simultaneously urge reform of

the Common Agricultural Policy, and the creation of a real common market in airfares, services, insurance, banking, and other services—when, at the same time, they secretly allow the other national governments to cast unofficial vetoes against these objectives.

It is paradoxical that the government in Britain proudly boasts of "strong government" while it simultaneously supports the ineffective decision-making process of the Council of Ministers. There could hardly be a more glaring example of weak government than the Council of Ministers—so why have Britain's national leaders supported it? The paradox is easily explained: both standpoints, although opposite to each other, are convenient to the leaders of the major parties in the House of Commons. Yet another illustration of national politicians putting their own advantage before that of the public.

The practice of majority voting in the Council of Ministers would surely benefit the British people. From time to time the British would lose a vote, but very much more often we would win them. Not only does Britain already possess ten votes towards the required blocking minority, but eleven times out of twelve we should not be the isolated country which was objecting to a proposed change. Strong service industries in Britain—such as banking, insurance and airlines—would benefit hugely from Community decisions. But decisions can only come through majority voting and not by giving secret vetoes to reluctant continental governments. It is time our national government ended its secret hypocrisy.

WHY THE BRITISH VETO WAS OVERRULED IN 1982

Perhaps the only knowledge of the veto possessed by the British public is the occasion in May 1982 when the British veto was overruled by the other nine Community governments. What happened has never been fully explained to the British public.

The problem arose in April 1982 when the Argentinians invaded the Falkland Islands. Immediately President Mitterand of France organised a unanimous embargo by all ten Community countries against exports of military equipment to Argentina and against all imports from Argentina. The embargo was arranged to last for one month initially and would be renewed if necessary. During the following month while sanctions against Argentina were applied fully by our partners, Britain's agriculture ministers were in Brussels to negotiate the annual changes in agricultural support prices for farmers (which are due at the end of

March every year because of inflation and other cost changes during the previous twelve months). The ten Agriculture ministers, *including our own*, unanimously agreed on new agricultural support prices. However, at the final moment, the British imposed a veto against formal ratification of the new prices: they did this in order to try to settle a separate British complaint, for a rebate from the annual Community Budget.

To the continental member states, this was a typical example of Perfidious Albion. The British were asking for, and were getting, full economic sanctions by the continentals against Argentinian exports. The jobs of people on the continent were being put at risk in order to help the British fight a war. But at the same time, as the continentals saw it, the British were withholding from continental farmers an overdue and *agreed* price adjustment following cost increases during the previous year. To a continental politician this was an impossible situation: the British could not have it both ways. The continentals agreed to renew the Community sanctions against Argentina for only one more week. The European Parliament held an emergency debate and accepted an amendment from this author (which was supported by a majority of those British Conservatives who voted) that Britain's attempted veto over agricultural prices should be overruled. The European Parliament cut the Gordian knot by recommending that both the agricultural prices should be put into effect and that the vital sanctions against Argentina should be continued. The Council of Ministers acted on the Parliament's recommendation and overruled the injudicious British attempt to use an unofficial veto. Sanctions by the Community against Argentina were renewed without a time limit. Meanwhile the Irish and Italian governments were experiencing pressures inside their own countries which prevented them from participating in sanctions again, but both gave undertakings not to undermine the Community sanctions.

HOW CAN NATIONAL MINISTERS BE FORCED TO TAKE DECISIONS?
It is clear that if the decision-making process in the Council of Ministers is not improved, then the British public, and the public throughout Europe, will not experience the benefits which they expect from our belonging to the European Community.

How can the ministers' decision making procedure be improved, so that real benefits come through to the public? Fortunately, there are a number of encouraging signs. Some percipient national leaders see the need for change. Herr Genscher, the German Foreign Minister, on 29th June, 1983 told the European Parliament:

"The future of the Community will depend on whether we decide on majority decisions in the framework of the treaties. In a future Europe of the Twelve, the observance by certain Member States of the so-called "Luxembourg Compromise" would mean that the Community was blockading itself . . . Such backlogs of problems as those facing us now cannot be tolerated by the Community for ever."

President Mitterand of France told the European Parliament on 24th May, 1984:

"We have the unanimity rule, which is used far more than the Treaties suggest and even more than is provided for by the Luxembourg Compromise. How can the complex and diversified unit that the Community has become be governed by the rules of the Diet of the old Kingdom of Poland, where every member could block the decisions? We all know where that led. It is time we returned to a more normal and more promising way of doing things. The French Government, which was behind this Compromise, has already proposed that it be used only in specific cases. The more frequent practice of voting on important questions heralds a return to the Treaties."

Mrs. Thatcher, in the paper which she handed to the other heads of government at their Fontainebleau meeting in June 1984, acknowledged that all was not well. She said:

"The voting provisions of the Treaty must be fully honoured. Unanimity must be respected in all cases where the Treaty so provides. The same applies for majority voting. At the same time, Member States must be able to continue to insist, where a very important national interest is at stake, on discussion continuing until agreement is reached. But they should be required in each case to set out their reasons fully."

Because of these failures to respect the rules by the national ministers, the European Parliament took the Council of Ministers to the European Court of Justice at Luxembourg, the final arbiter on Community law. The Parliament asked for a ruling that the Council of Ministers had failed in its obligations by not deciding on overdue proposals, specifically on sixteen concerning the Common Transport Policy.

The British government's attitude to this court case was

characteristically bizarre. In the Court, it *opposed* the Parliament's complaint. But, subsequently, it has *welcomed* the verdict and said that the verdict supports its own views!

In May 1985 the European Court of Justice ruled as the European Parliament hoped—that the national ministers had indeed acted illegally. The national ministers may be forced to start voting by majority in order to obey the Court.

At last, there are signs that the benefits of belonging to the Community may start to flow through to the patiently waiting public.

However, there are still reasons to doubt the sincerity of these nice-sounding statements by national leaders that they will improve the behaviour of the Council of Ministers. In the summer of 1985, the German government were asked to accept a tiny decrease in the support price for cereal-growers (cereals being in huge surplus). The Germans refused and cast a veto against any reduction—and were supported by the British government!

CHAPTER FIVE

An Alarming Gap In Democratic Control

Democratic control of decisions made in the European Community is alarmingly *inadequate*.

There are two executive bodies in the Community to take the decisions and to carry them out. They are the Council of Ministers and the Commission. Both hold their meetings in secret. Neither is fully accountable to the public for their decisions.

THE COMMISSION

The Commission (the E.E.C.'s civil service) is run by "Commissioners" who are simultaneously *appointed* every four years by the heads of each of the national governments. (The two currently from Britain are Lord Cockfield and Stanley Clinton Davis: they were appointed by Mrs. Thatcher in January 1985.)

The public has no way to express its views about the choice of Commissioners. Even their elected representatives in the national parliament cannot alter the appointments, which are the gift of party leaders. Nor can the public vote directly for the appointment of a Commissioner—as the American public can when it elects a President.

However the Commission, as a body, is sensitive to these criticisms. It makes a deliberate effort to consult and to listen to the elected European Parliament—although it has the right (from the Treaty of Rome) to ignore the Parliament's views. The European Parliament has the formal power to vote to dismiss all the Commissioners together. It does not yet have a formal power to approve their appointment, although in 1985 it took upon itself to vote approval of them in any case.

THE COUNCIL OF MINISTERS ...

The Council of Ministers is a far more serious problem. It meets in secret. Neither the press, nor the public, nor members of the European Parliament can attend its meetings. In their secret meetings the national ministers or their civil servants habitually abuse the confidence of the public by awarding secret vetoes to each other. These secret vetoes, for the most part, have no legal basis—as we have seen in the previous chapter. Nor are the secret vetoes justified to the public afterwards.

... IS NOT CONTROLLABLE BY NATIONAL PARLIAMENTS

National parliaments are not able to control the activities of the Council of Ministers. This is accepted by the House of Commons, where only a small proportion of Community matters are debated. The few debates are usually held late at night, this timing being deliberately chosen by the ministers. The final motion after each debate is only to *take note* of the Community's decision because no national parliament has any power to alter even a single comma of most decisions by the Council of Ministers. The present normal procedure is that Council decisions are taken in secret, have immediate effect, and are not subject to parliamentary control!

... IS NOT CONTROLLED BY THE EUROPEAN PARLIAMENT WHICH CAN ONLY GIVE ITS OPINION

The democratic body in the Community, the elected European Parliament, only has the right to give an *opinion* on decisions which are made by the two executive bodies: it has no power to block decisions which it does not like. The Treaty of Rome lays down that the European Parliament has the right to be consulted, but—except over the annual E.E.C. Budget—it does not have the right to control the decisions of the Community's executive bodies.

TWO PARTICULAR EXAMPLES OF INADEQUATE CONTROL OF THE COUNCIL OF MINISTERS

One disgraceful example of undemocratic behaviour is the habit of secret and unofficial vetoes in the Council of Ministers—of which the public is ignorant and which delay the benefits which they expect.

A second example of the lack of adequate control is the Common Agricultural Policy (the C.A.P.). This is not controlled by any parliament at all, either national or European! National parliaments do not control the C.A.P. because the final power of decision lies in the Council of Ministers: when the Ministers of Agriculture from the twelve member states reach a decision, it is final and from that moment is not subject to change by national parliaments.

Nor, despite its real powers over the Community's Budget, can the European Parliament control agricultural spending although it would be the obvious forum for control. It cannot control the spending on agriculture because of a peculiarity in the Treaty of Rome: in that document agricultural spending is classified as "compulsory", whereas most non-agricultural spending is classified as "non-compulsory". For "compulsory" spending, the Council of Ministers is given the final say: for "non-compulsory" spending the Parliament has the final say.

Consequently, the final say about spending on the Common Agricultural Policy is given to decision-makers who meet in secret and whose decisions cannot afterwards be challenged by any parliament! No wonder the Common Agricultural Policy is out of control.

THE PRINCIPLE OF SAFEGUARDS FOR DEMOCRACY
An essential safeguard for stable democracy is that there should be adequate democratic control and proper separation of the powers of government. In other words, the different powers of government should be kept separate instead of being concentrated in too few hands. Each separate power should be subject to full democratic control.

Curiously, we do not enjoy these safeguards to the full in the United Kingdom. In Westminster both the executive and the legislative arms of government are controlled by the same person, the Prime Minister. This leader becomes in effect a short term dictator between elections (for as long as he or she retains the confidence of their closest supporters) because they control both the decision-making machinery and the people's representatives (who should be controlling the decision-makers).

The founding fathers of the new United States of America, when splitting away from Britain two hundred years ago, deliberately and wisely separated the powers of their own government. As a result, today's elected American President selects his own cabinet members who become responsible for the day-to-day executive decisions of government. But the decisions of the President and of his Cabinet are subject to the final and absolute approval of the two directly elected houses of Congress, the Senate and the House of Representatives.

SHOULD WE WORRY?
Why should we worry about this inadequate democratic control of Community decision-making? We should definitely be concerned

because the fundamental principle of separate democratic control of each of the powers does not exist in the European Community. The Commission and the Council of Ministers have executive powers: but the public's representatives in the elected Parliament have only the right to be consulted for an opinion rather than being able to withhold powers from the executive if that is necessary in the public interest.

HOW TO RESTORE FULL DEMOCRATIC CONTROL IN THE COMMUNITY?

A change needs to be made so that there is full control over the secret decision-makers. So, who should be exerting full democratic control over the secret decision-makers of the Community?

It would be impossible for the multitude of Community decisions, many smallscale, to be referred for approval to all twelve national parliaments. To have twelve separate national parliaments trying to agree promptly together on amendments would be impossible. In any case this would impose such an extra workload that it would completely block their own national responsibilities.

The only possible candidate to carry out proper democratic control of executive decisions in the Community is the European Parliament. It is fully democratic, being directly elected by the public every five years.

But the European Parliament's present right only to be consulted—and then to frequently see its opinion ignored by the Council of Ministers—is inadequate, is insulting to the public, and is potentially dangerous to democracy.

RESPONSIBILITY FOR CONTROL SHOULD HAVE BEEN GIVEN IN 1979

Prior to the first direct elections in 1979, the Parliament was composed of national M.P.s who were sent from each national parliament. They were under the control of the national leaders who sent them to Strasbourg for a few pleasant days each month. But although full democratic legitimacy was conferred on the European Parliament by the first direct European elections in 1979, responsibility for control of the executive decisions was not transferred at the same time—and the principle of separation of powers was not respected by the national leaders who made the arrangements.

Responsibilities for decision-making have been transferred to the Community by national parliaments in many fields: in foreign relations, (for example the ratification of international treaties such as the G.A.T.T. and the C.S.C.E.): in the customs union (external trade policy and setting of levels of external duties): in the Common Agricultural Policy: in competition policy (the granting of subsidies to ailing national industries): in powers to harmonise taxation: in transport (setting of quotas for lorry movements between member states); and so on. But while power to make decisions has been transferred from national governments to the Community, the power to control the decisions had been lost by national parliaments and has not been correspondingly transferred to the European Parliament.

NO TRANSFER OF POWERS AWAY FROM NATIONAL PARLIAMENTS IS NEEDED

The European Parliament does not need to take any powers away from the national parliaments of the member states in order to correct this situation. It simply needs *an increase in its responsibilities* in order that the executive decisions of the Council of Ministers and of the Commission shall be made subject to separate and full democratic control.

Why are certain national leaders in the Community—including Britain's leader—*opposed* to this increase in responsibility for the European Parliament? The answer is simple: it is because their own personal power would become more subject to control, which is something they would not enjoy!

CHAPTER SIX

Next Steps in the Community's Development?

The doubts which the public have about British membership of the European Community are caused not only by the apparent lack of immediate benefits, but also because they have not been given any clear view of the end-goal with the benefits that eventual unification of Europe should bring.

In the early postwar years after 1945 the immediate goal was to find a way to guarantee "peace within Europe". No country in Europe could afford a third civil war in Europe: all had been hugely weakened by two such wars already in the twentieth century. That goal has been achieved. War between any of the countries in western Europe is now unthinkable. But a new challenge has arisen.

Now the challenge is for the peoples who live in the European corner of the world to work together effectively in order to keep themselves free, democratic and independent in the face of the superpowers elsewhere in the world. Working together offers the best prospect for future generations of Europeans including the British. Neither Britain no any other European nation has sufficient resources of its own any longer to be able to compete with the world's superpowers economically, militarily or politically.

There is therefore a continuing momentum towards unification in Europe while preserving the rich variety of customs and traditions. This is a process that began over thirty years ago.

"AN EVER CLOSER UNION"
The signatories to the Treaty of Rome committed their countries in its first preamble to be "determined to lay the foundations of an *ever closer union* among the peoples of Europe". This committment has been

reaffirmed many times since. When Mrs. Thatcher and the nine national heads of government met at Stuttgart in June 1983 they unanimously reconfirmed in writing their "commitment to progress toward an ever closer union among the peoples and member states of the European Community". Mrs. Thatcher and the British Conservative party are thus committed to "ever closer union" among the peoples of Europe.

For the British people to take a share in "ever closer union" will be a major but worthwhile step but it will mean having to shed some of their traditional national arrangements. It may be an appropriate analogy that, on reaching maturity, men and women marry in order to share wider responsibilities and privileges: the alternative being to remain single, to consume one's own resources and in due course to die out. The nation state has become gradually less adequate to deal with new problems as the twentieth century has progressed. The benefits to the British people of joining a wider European union—more rights, more opportunities, and greater security—are desirable in themselves, fully consistent with Conservative philosophy, and are necessary if we are to meet the challenges of a fast-changing world.

NEXT STEP, A NEW TREATY?

The most recent formal attempt to map the next steps towards a united Europe was produced by the European Parliament in February 1984. It was a new draft Treaty to lead on from the Treaty of Rome. The document was the brainchild of an Italian M.E.P., Altiero Spinelli. The Parliament's purpose was to try to give a new impetus to European unification which had been slowing down.

The European Parliament's main proposals were as follows:

1. In order to get decisions made effectively—instead of the present logjam which deprives the public of benefits—the Council of Ministers should take its decisions by majority votes. As an exception, during the first ten years votes may be postponed if a member state claims that it has a genuinely vital national interest, providing the objector's reasons are published.

2. In order to ensure that the Community remains fully and democratically accountable, the elected European Parliament should have increased responsibility over the appointment and the work programme of the Commission (the Community's civil service); joint decision-making over legislation with the Council of Ministers; the

right to propose new Community laws and the abolition of the unnecessary distinction between "compulsory" and "non-compulsory" spending in the Community's Budget.

3. European Monetary Union:
There should be progressive moves towards full monetary union in Europe including a European federal responsibility for monetary and credit policies, the creation of a European Monetary Fund with authority and responsibility to guarantee monetary stability.

4. To be able to create new Common Policies by making national laws compatible with each other although not necessarily identical; to agree common standards for telecommunications; and where appropriate to create policies in other fields, such as Defence, providing that all member state parliaments agree.

Some of these steps appear to be too large for all twelve national governments to be able to take unanimously together. Consequently there might be a danger that nothing at all would be the result. At the summit in Milan in June 1985 three national leaders were reluctant to agree to new steps: Greece (partly because its government relies on communist support), Denmark (whose leader has been a European federalist for many years but who leads a minority government) and Britain (with its traditional negative attitude to new ideas). The other member states are not deterred by the reluctance of the minority. They are aware that most European developments have come from certain states setting a lead with others following later. The British must hope that our leaders have learned the lesson of 1957 and will not allow us to be excluded again from the writing of the rules.

ATTITUDES TO FURTHER UNION IN THE MEMBER STATES

The document was a draft which was sent to all the national parliaments in the Community in order to obtain their suggestions for improvements. All the national parliaments except one debated the draft.

For France, President Mitterand sketched his views in a speech to the European Parliament in May 1984 in these words:

"A new situation calls for a new treaty which must not, of course, be a substitute for existing treaties, but an extension of them to fields they do not currently cover. This is the case with the European Political Community. France, ladies and gentlemen, is available for such an enterprise. I, on its behalf, state its willingness to examine and defend your project, the inspiration behind which it approves."

Chancellor Kohl of the Federal Republic of Germany has often and publicly expressed his belief in the goal of an eventual United States of Europe.

The Italian national parliament was the first in the member states to welcome the Spinelli document.

The Belgian parliament called on its own government to open negotiations on the new draft treaty.

The Danish Conservative party has had the goal of European Union in its election manifesto for several national elections in Denmark. Although it does not yet have a majority in the national Danish parliament, the Conservatives are in the ascendant and may soon achieve a majority.

The British remained doubtful. There was no formal debate in the House of Commons. Even the British M.E.P.s in the European Parliament were uncertain about it: when the draft Treaty was approved at Strasbourg in February 1984 it received a total of two hundred and thirty-one votes in favour, with thirty-one against and forty-four abstentions. The eighty-one British M.E.P.s were very divided: twenty-three voted in favour (twenty-two Conservatives including the author, plus one from the S.D.P.), twelve voted against (six Conservatives, six Labour), nine abstained (five Conservatives, three Labour, and one from Northern Ireland): but thirty-seven stayed away from the vote altogether!

It is very important that Britain's national government does not ignore the new proposals, hoping like an ostrich with its head in the sand that if it ignores them then they may go away. We cannot veto the proposals, and to ignore them could lead to our exclusion again from new developments in Europe—just as we have always done to ourselves ever since 1945, and always to our subsequent regret. Most of the other Community nations would not wish to see the British fall behind and be left in the second division. But the House of Commons must not assume that the other nations will not dare, in the last resort, to move ahead towards European union and leave us behind. In the last resort, if absolutely necessary, they will—and we could not prevent them.

In retrospect, it is clear that when the British boycotted the founding of the Common Market in 1957, we locked ourselves out of the exceptional economic growth which was enjoyed by the six founding member states. By locking ourselves out at the start, we also made it exceedingly difficult to later achieve changes in the Common Agricultural Policy.

Those who oppose the new proposals seriously underestimate the need to improve the existing procedures of the Community. The Treaty of Rome was drawn up over a quarter of a century ago. The need for changes is obvious when the Community has still not eliminated all internal barriers to trade between the member states so as to create a true common market. The abolition of trade barriers would be greatly to the advantage of Britain, which has more industry and services to offer whereas most other member states have more agriculture.

THE FINAL SHAPE OF UNITED EUROPE: A DEGREE OF FEDERALISM?
The final shape of United Europe will be whatever proves to suit Europeans best. It will not be a direct copy of any other system of government elsewhere in the world, for example of the federal systems in the United States or Switzerland nor of the successful federal systems set up by British governments in former colonies including Australia or Canada.

"Federalism" has become an unfashionable word among Britain's national politicians. Presumably that is because they feel threatened by the idea. But the Conservative party prides itself above all on being a pragmatic party. It should therefore be willing to examine openmindedly every possibility including federalism for improving the life of the British people.

As for any other union, it will be necessary for Europe to have a central or federal governing body with sufficient powers to enact and to enforce European-scale decisions. This central decision making will have to be balanced by the maximum delegation of powers to the national parliaments of the individual member states.

Central governments in successful federal states have control over foreign policy, defence, currency and money supply, postal and communication services and partially over internal security.

A DIRECTLY-ELECTED EUROPEAN PRESIDENT?
The President of a European federal system might be directly elected by the public—as is done in the United States of America.

A TWO CHAMBER EUROPEAN PARLIAMENT?
A federal European government might be controlled by Europe's own form of a double chamber parliament. The lower house might be

the present European Parliament, answerable directly to the public. The upper house might consist of representatives of the individual states, as does the United States' Senate in Washington D.C. A proposal could be blocked by either chamber of the parliament but not by an individual member nor by an individual state.

Confronted with these ideas the British may feel alarmed. They may ask whether this might mean the end of the British Parliament, and perhaps even of the monarchy? The answer to both questions is "most definitely not". One of the most vital sections embodied in the European Parliament's draft Treaty, is an important principle with the unattractive name of Subsidiarity.

THE SUBSIDIARITY PRINCIPLE WHICH PROTECTS NATIONAL PARLIAMENTS

"Subsidiarity" means the *maximum delegation* of powers to the level of government as near as possible to the public. The draft Treaty proposes that the European Union "shall only act to carry out those tasks which may be undertaken more effectively in common than by the Member States acting separately".

In other words that, a federal European government and Parliament would only take over responsibility from national parliaments for matters which extended beyond national boundaries and which, it was agreed, were best dealt with on a European scale. The national British parliament will continue to decide purely internal British questions such as whether we drive on the left or the right of the road, and whether we have restricted opening hours for our public houses. This principle of maximum delegation of powers guarantees the continued and essential existence of national parliaments including Westminster.

NO THREAT TO OUR MONARCHY EITHER

There is no suggestion that member states must become republics in order to join a federal Europe. Indeed there are six monarchies among the twelve Community countries.

NEW COMMON POLICIES, SUCH AS DEFENCE

There are many areas which the European Community does not cover. Defence is an obvious candidate. The Americans are becoming increasingly reluctant to continue to have to pay so large a share for the defence of our continent when we Europeans are as rich as they. Europe will have to pay more for its own defence. It is an interesting rumour that the Americans are trying to push the neutral Southern Irish into joining N.A.T.O., in return for which their price is said to be the reunification of the Irish island.

AN EVEN LARGER COMMUNITY?
The next prospects for joining the Community are the E.F.T.A. countries. Also, Morocco has made a formal request to join, but its geographical qualifications are not very good.

Looking much further ahead, a United Europe should include the countries now under Soviet occupation in East Europe—Poland, Czechoslovakia, Hungary, Yugoslavia and East Germany. The criteria for joining the European Community are to be European, to be democratic, and to be willing to adhere to the Treaties. But it is recognised that these countries will take some time before they are free to join.

One other prospect is Turkey. This country belongs to N.A.T.O. and to the Council of Europe, and it has incorporated the European Convention of Human Rights into its own law. But its population is likely to reach one hundred million by the turn of the century and the expense of financing so many backward people is a truly daunting one for the Community.

RECONCILIATION OF DIFFERENCES
It is to be hoped that the growing together of the European peoples may contribute to reconciliation over regional differences and territorial disputes—such as the Basque problem, language problems in Belgium, Spanish claims to Gibraltar, mistrust between Greece and Turkey, the religious differences in Northern Ireland, and the re-unification of East and West Germany.

THE PROBLEM OF TOO MANY EUROPEAN LANGUAGES
There is one area in which it is seems unlikely that there can be much progress. That is the problem of too many languages in Europe. There are now nine official languages spoken in the Community countries—and many other unofficial ones.

No individual nation is willing—understandably—to give up using its own native language because that would lead eventually to the death of its literature and of its culture. Unless there is an unforseen technological linguistic breakthrough, or unless we all make a successful effort to learn each other's languages, it will be necessary to continue for many more years with expensive translation services. But translation expenses are a small price to pay for reconciliation between the peoples of Europe. Our continent is neither the best or worst off in this respect. Most fortunate is North America where one official language is spoken and South America with only two. Worse off is India where there are fifteen official languages.

In the long run, the Community's nine official languages may divide into major and minor ones. In the Council of Europe, which is the debating society without powers for the twenty-one democratic countries of Europe, only two languages are used, English and French. But to use only two in a Community with real powers is not acceptable to the smaller members states. In the meantime, a greater effort must be made to make an effort to teach our children a second, and even a third language.

OUR INTERESTS ARE GREATER THAN OUR DIFFERENCES
There are many problems that divide us in Europe, and there probably always will be—just as there continue to be problems inside Britain. But the common interests that are shared by all the peoples of western Europe—the preservation of our liberties, our traditions and our ways of life—are very much greater than our differences.

It is difficult for all Europeans is to recognise that circumstances are changing, that old arrangements are not necessarily the most suitable for the future, that the nation state is becoming inadequate for dealing with modern problems, and that we have to pool our resources if future generations of Europe are to remain free.

WHAT ABOUT OUR SOVEREIGNTY?
Many British people fear, however, that if we pool some of our resources with the other Europeans, whom we have traditionally distrusted, then we shall lose our sovereignty and that the British way of life will be threatened. This fear is examined in the next chapter.

CHAPTER SEVEN

Sovereignty, The Misunderstood Concept

Another version of this choice which faces the British is whether we should take a share in the greater sovereignty of a united Europe or whether we prefer our own sovereignty, shrinking but British, a small thing but our own (to adapt Shakespeare).

A fear commonly voiced in Britain is that we may be "losing our sovereignty" by belonging to the European Community. People fear that the British way of life is threatened. However, closer examination suggests that these fears are untrue; indeed the opposite appears more likely to be true—that our traditions are better protected being inside a strong Community than being outside and alone.

"THE BRITISH WAY OF LIFE" IS NOT THREATENED BY THE EUROPEAN COMMUNITY.

Many years after Britain joined the Community in 1973, we still have our Queen; we continue to eat sliced bread and to drink warm beer; our police are unarmed; we drive on the left of the road; we are not forced to carry identity cards; we vote on Thursdays; milk is delivered in pints to our doorsteps (which is threatened, not by Brussels, but because we drink less every year and because British dairies have chosen to sell milk through supermarkets); our public houses are open at the restricted times that we have chosen; we have our own civil and criminal laws; we have Greenwich Mean Time; we play cricket and snooker; the Pope has not interfered with our national churches; imported animals are subject to quarantine to keep out rabies; and so on. Nor have there been any Community proposals to change these habits, despite deliberately mischievous rumours by opponents of our continuing membership.

Recent controversial changes in the habits of the British people have been decided voluntarily by ourselves. The Community did not ask us to decimalise our currency in 1971; the decision to change to selling petrol by litres at garages instead of by gallons was made by the oil companies; our weather forecasters have voluntarily changed to speaking of temperature in Centigrade instead of in Fahrenheit.

Nor do other European peoples appear to have lost their own traditions since the Community began in 1957. The Italians continue to eat spaghetti, still drive recklessly, and still wave their hands about when they speak. The French continue to eat snails and frogs' legs; they still force-feed geese in order to turn their livers into pâté: and their logic is still maddening in British eyes.

The old joke still seems to be true that the "perfect" Euro-bureaucrat has the humility of a Frenchman, the punctuality of an Italian, the wit of a German and the linguistic skill of an Englishman.

Indeed wherever one looks the opposite of the fear seems to be true. Traditions and cultures are best preserved from a position of strength. There are too many peoples who are living in the Russian empire today who are paying a high price for their grandfathers' confidence that their little nations could remain both small, isolated and free. Even so, some of their traditions survive.

OUR INTERESTS ARE BETTER PROTECTED FROM INSIDE THE COMMUNITY

Many British activities are profoundly influenced by events elsewhere in the world. Our interests are protected better against these pressures by the combined strength of the Community than they could be by ourselves alone.

Our imports and exports are dependent on the terms of the General Agreement on Tariffs and Trades. Favourable quotas and tariffs are negotiated by the European Community on our behalf but with greater muscle power than we could find alone. Our sovereignty is greater.

Economic sanctions against the Argentinians in 1982 were effective because the whole Community applied them together: British sanctions alone would have achieved much less. This cohesion should not be taken for granted; in 1973 the Dutch were abandoned by their fellow Community members when the Arab oil exporters applied a boycott. Again, by acting together in the dispute about the natural gas pipeline from Siberia, Community countries preserved British and continental jobs by obliging the Americans to relent when they tried to force companies to cancel their already-signed contracts. The British alone could not have resisted the American pressure to cancel. Our sovereignty was greater.

For Defence, British membership of N.A.T.O. means than we are safer than if we were isolated. Supreme control over our armed forces in the European theatre now rests in the hands of an American Supreme Commander who can commit British forces to counter a Russian attack on Germany. Our sovereignty is greater.

Our Human Rights are guaranteed by the European Convention on Human Rights. It is enforced by the European Court on Human Rights at Strasbourg. British people may sue there as individuals if they believe that their rights are being infringed. The British government is obliged to obey the judgements of the Court. This court is separate from the Community but is another example of how the rights of the British are strengthened by a sharing of sovereignty.

THE TRUE DEFINITION OF SOVEREIGNTY

The Oxford dictionary defines the meaning of "Sovereign" as "supreme and exempt from external control".

In Queen Victoria's reign the British probably were "supreme and exempt from external control": but today we have no empire and we are subject to all sorts of world pressures. (When British football supporters helped to cause a riot in Brussels, we could not avoid our soccer clubs being banned from international competitions).

If we were isolated, the British people would not have as much sovereignty as they have now. If we were isolated we would be increasingly vulnerable to external pressures as our importance in the world continues to decline.

Britain is not sovereign economically. As long ago as 1956 we were forced into unwilling withdrawal from Suez by American pressure on sterling. We have also been forced into economic change from outside in recent years by the International Monetary Fund and by OPEC's oil price increases. In 1985 our currency fell and rose like a yo-yo at the whim of the world's financial speculators.

The sovereignty of the British is increased if they are part of a strong and democratic Community. The European Community is a safer place for the British people to be than living in a isolated from the mainstream.

It is incorrect for the British people to talk of "surrender of sovereignty" because we belong to the European Community. Instead it is accurate to talk of "a pooling of sovereignty" or of "our share in a greater European sovereignty".

WESTMINSTER'S OWN SHRINKING SOVEREIGNTY

How has this misunderstanding by the British people of the concept of their sovereignty come about? The sovereignty of the British people is not at risk so long as they live democratically. The misunderstanding about sovereignty surely arises because it is the sovereignty of the British national *parliament* which is shrinking. This is borne out if one observes who is voicing the fears about national sovereignty: the fears are voiced by Westminster politicians who blame the European Community for their own decline.

There is a danger that our national British politicians are putting their own interests at Westminister above the interests of the British people. For example, a senior Conservative M.P. told Conservative M.E.P.s including the author at the start of March 1983 that there would not, *under any circumstances*, be an increase in Britain's gross V.A.T. payment to the European Community (in other words, an increase in our gross payments beyond the existing one per cent of V.A.T.) whether or not that brought greater returns and benefits to the British people! Why? Because, it was specifically stated by the explainee, an increased gross V.A.T. payment to Brussels would be a transfer of Westminster's sovereignty. (It was therefore gratifying to see that our Prime Minister agreed at the June 1984 summit at Fontainebleau to increase the ceiling on gross British V.A.T. payments from 1 per cent to 1.4 per cent before our rebate.)

It is true that our sharing in the greater European sovereignty will threaten some of our national British institutions. Those threatened will include our British passport and customs officers. The public has been brainwashed by government into forgetting that these are devices for *limiting* their freedoms. The European Parliament looks forward to the day when all such restrictions on movements by British and other European citizens *inside* the Community will have been abolished.

OUR REAL CHOICE ABOUT SOVEREIGNTY

The choice about sovereignty is not understood by the British public. They can gain a share in a greater sovereignty inside the European Community rather than clinging to a gradually vanishing island sovereignty.

The interests of the British public and the interests of their national Parliament are no longer identical. However, there is a profound difficulty about explaining this variation in sovereignty to the public because it is the *national politicians* in the House of Commons who still dominate the attention of the British media—newspapers, television, and radio.

Almost no senior Westminster politician sees a reward for him or herself in explaining to the public about our unavoidable involvement in the unification of Europe.

AN ACUTE DILEMMA FOR THE BRITISH

There is thus an acute dilemma: a change in the British public's understanding about the Community is necessary before they can draw more benefits from our membership. But this change in understanding is dependent on efforts by our national leaders at Westminster; and our national leaders see their own personal interests in having no change in the British public's lack of understanding. What is to be done to cut this Gordian knot? The next chapter suggests some answers.

CHAPTER EIGHT

We Could Get Much More Out Of The Community

Hopefully, the reader accepts that we cannot afford to leave the Community. As major exporters we need to have *guaranteed* free access to the Common Market, and we need to remain members to keep our "say" in the writing of the rules.

Further steps towards unification along Churchill's proposed lines are intended by a majority of the other member states of the Community. In order to retain our "say" about these developments we must continue to be fully involved. If we do not, we risk being relegated to a lower division of the Community where we will be forced to watch European decisions which affect us being made without our voice.

So, if we must involve ourselves in the activities of the Community, should we not put in the greatest possible effort in order to take out the most possible benefits?

OUR PRESENT "COULD NOT CARE LESS" ATTITUDE IS
HARMFUL TO US

There are very many ways in which we currently miss out on potential benefits from our membership. The present British national attitude to the European Community is that it does not matter very much, that we need not bother about it very much, that ignoring it does not matter very much, and if we ignore it for long enough, with luck it might even shrivel away altogether and leave us alone. The consequence of this "could not care less" attitude is that we miss out on many benefits to which our membership entitles us.

We should accept that the European Community is here to stay, and therefore that Britain's membership is here to stay. We should accept that Britain's role and the British parliament's role in the world are much reduced by the loss of empire. Then we can discover the role which Dean Acheson long ago demonstrated that we were seeking and move towards the leadership of a uniting Europe.

WHO WILL EXPLAIN THIS TO THE BRITISH PUBLIC?

This necessity of "thinking European" has to start from leaders in all sectors of our society—parliament, industry, the churches, the trade unions, the teachers, the journalists, and so on. But the primary lead has to come from the party leaders at Westminster because their speeches are given most prominence by the media.

It may be asked why Britain's M.E.P.s do not do more to publicise the case? The answer is that they try to do so. But, except possibly for Sir Henry Plumb and Lady Castle, they are not even minor national names whose views can command the media's attention. The British press has become preoccupied with a frantic search for sales and ratings at the expense of facts. Their priority has become Entertainment rather than Information. The subject of "Europe" does not sell newspapers nor attract viewers to the television screen and it is therefore ignored.

Nor do M.E.P.s have sufficient means to provide the information even to all their own constituents. M.E.P.s represent over half a million voters each, eight times as many as each M.P. at Westminster. Yet M.E.P.s receive the same salary and not dissimilar expenses to M.P.s. The true parallel for an M.E.P. is not an M.P. at Westminster but a member of the House of Representatives in Washington D.C. Like M.E.P.s, the latter each represents about half a million voters—but each is able to employ up to eighteen full-time assistants and can mail free a bulletin four times per year to every one of their constituents. If M.E.P.s had equivalent facilities they could inform the public about the importance of taking Europe seriously.

It therefore depends on Britain's national leaders at Westminster. The change to a positive attitude by the British about Europe has to come initially from leading national politicians because they command the British media's attention. They should be presenting European policy in positive terms which the public can understand.

Until now, the British public has been told only about arguments with the Community—but nothing about its long-term goals. The public only knows the details of our annual rebates from the Community's budget but not how relatively small they are (£0.5 billion) compared to the national British budget (£130 billion in 1985-6), and about food surpluses and cheap butter to the Russians, but not that our government allows other governments to cast a secret veto against the necessary reforms.

Sadly, there is a major doubt whether our national leaders are willing to do what is necessary. It was significant that not a single senior member of the Conservative government made a speech in favour of "Europe" during the European election campaign of May-June 1984: instead they made personal appearances at daily press conferences at their party headquarters—at which, not unexpectedly, journalists questioned them about Westminster issues!

"CATCH 22"

The problem about getting the public to make the most of Europe is that it is the same Westminster leaders who are obliged to accept the shrinking importance of their role in order to encourage understanding in the British public about the benefits obtainable from the uniting of Europe.

With the Community, as for electoral reform, the strongest resistance to change comes from the very national politicians who have the powers to bring about the changes, they being the principal beneficiaries of the present negative attitudes.

What should our national leaders do? The Labour party is dying, although it has enough vigour to entertain the public with its hara-kiri act for some time to come. However the leaders of the Conservatives and of the other parties at Westminster, should set a lead by educating the public in a positive way about the European Community. It is disappointing that the two Alliance parties, which claim to be the most European-minded, make so little attempt to explain the benefits of Europe to the British public.

Educating the public means admitting that decisions cannot be taken effectively by twelve national ministers in the Council of Ministers if they always seek to be unanimous: that instead there has to be a European decision-making mechanism which will be separate from national parliaments; and that sometimes, but not often if we argue our British case well, we shall be outvoted on minor issues but that in return majority voting means that the British public will at last obtain the benefits which have been blocked by some of the continentals.

Educating the public means explaining that we already receive a wide range of benefits from Europe but that we could receive many more; that membership means more than merely the size of the annual rebate which Mrs. Thatcher squeezes out of the Community's little Budget. (The Community's annual Budget equals one per cent of the combined budgets of the national governments.)

THE DAMAGE CAUSED BY "I WANT MY MONEY BACK"
Although Mrs. Thatcher fortunately has stopped using her damaging statement, "I want my money back," her remark did enormous harm to the British interests and left an indelible impression on continental as well as on British public opinion. The damage lay in the message that it conveyed—that Britain's current leader only saw the Community in terms of pounds and pence instead of the benefits that it brought (peace, increased trade, etc.). It also revealed her ignorance that it was the Community's money, not Britain's, which she was demanding to have back. (Customs Duties and one per cent of Value Added Tax were made over to the European Community when we joined in 1973.)

THE COMMONS SHOULD START TO TAKE AN INTEREST IN EUROPE
There is very little understanding of Community matters in the House of Commons—except for the tiny number of ex-M.E.P.s and a few enthusiasts. Europe is thought of as something remote, irritating (late-night debates), difficult, and unlikely to bring short-term popularity to any M.P. It is the responsibility of the *Foreign* Office—which itself suggests that "Europe" is foreign instead of being a part of our everyday life.

The House of Commons should seek ways of genuinely understanding European proposals. Their present innate scepticism about European proposals is a healthy way to test their value, but scepticism should not be reinforced by bias and ignorance. If Westminster's M.P.s do not understand European proposals, how can the public be helped to understand? The House of Lords is vastly superior in its careful and selective appraisal of European proposals.

NO FORMAL LIAISON BETWEEN BRITISH M.P.s AND M.E.P.s...
There could to be a joint committee between British M.P.s and M.E.P.s (whose knowledge and understanding of developments in Europe is infinitely deeper than that of any Westminster M.P.). A notable example on this has already been set by the German national parliament, the Bundestag, which has a joint standing committee between its national M.P.s and its European representatives in order that each side is well informed of the other's views and experiences.

... AND MINIMAL INFORMATION LIAISON
For informal liaison between M.P.s and M.E.P.s, the contrast between Britain and the continent is equally unfavourable. German

M.E.P.s receive full office facilities in the Bundestag and are encouraged to liaise closely with their opposite numbers. Danish Conservative M.E.P.s are given equal facilities with the national Conservative M.P.s in the Folketing the Danish parliament. But at Westminster whereas unpaid American research students working for M.P.s can freely enter the House of Commons and may use the research library, British M.E.P.s before entering are *searched* each time by policemen for explosives or weapons and may not use the library. No British M.E.P. has an office facility or is permitted to even buy an occasional drink for an M.P. in the House of Commons. It is no wonder that British M.E.P.s visit the House of Commons less frequently than they should.

THE GOVERNMENT'S DAMAGING RELUCTANCE TO HEED
ADVICE FROM ITS OWN M.E.P.s

The British government, by ignoring the advice of M.E.P.s and insisting on playing its European hand in its own way, twice triggered the European Parliament into withholding the British 1983 rebate. This happened as follows:

In October 1983 the Council of Ministers was still unwilling to agree on overdue but vital reforms to the Common Agricultural Policy. The major political groups in the European Parliament, including the Conservatives, drafted a package of financial sanctions in order to increase pressure on the indecisive Council of Ministers. Their sanctions included withholding both agricultural funds and the British and German rebates. The Parliament's purpose was to squeeze the Council of Ministers into deciding on painful, urgent and long overdue reforms to the agricultural surpluses—and in this respect its purpose exactly agreed with the British government.

The European Parliament's draft sanctions included a written guarantee that no measure would be taken by the European Parliament that would penalise any one member state and not the others: this draft delighted the Conservative M.E.P.s who realised that the British rebate would not be singled out for withholding all by itself. They forsaw that our rebate must be withheld during the first reading of the Budget as part of the Parliament's package of sanctions—but knew that our rebate would be released more *rapidly* subsequently because it was part of the package.

However a message came from the British government in London to the Conservative M.E.P.s at Strasbourg that they should not vote in favour of the sanctions package against the Council of Ministers even on the first reading because London knew best. The Conservative M.E.P.s were divided, some deciding to follow London out of loyalty, others knowing it was bad advice because our rebate would be singled out for withholding if they now abandoned the package. Finally the Conservative group decided by a narrow majority to follow London's instructions out of loyalty and because next year was election year: except for three (one being the author) they voted against the European Parliament's package of sanctions. The immediate consequence was that the continental M.E.P.s viewed the British as traitors—and therefore singled out the British rebate for withholding.

The rebate was still being withheld in July 1984. At the summit of national leaders at Fontainebleau in June 1984 it had been agreed, although unfortunately not in writing, that the Community's cash shortfall in the autumn of 1984 (caused by the Council of Ministers' indecision about cutting back milk over-production) would have to be met by extra finance from all ten national governments. Immediately after the summit, Westminster announced, in a clumsy negotiating ploy to try to force extra economies in agricultural spending, that they would not pay another penny to help with the cash shortfall. The continentals were incensed—and the European Parliament at its next session in July immediately voted to continue to withhold the British 1983 rebate. Subsequently the British government announced that it would, of course after all, pay its share towards the 1984 cash shortfall. The British rebate was released by the European Parliament. But not before the British government had again inflicted wounds on itself by failing to listen to its own Conservative M.E.P.s.

WESTMINSTER DOES NOT UTILISE BRITISH EXPERIENCE IN EUROPE...
The process of selection of the two Commissioners from Britain to serve in Brussels is far from satisfactory. All British governments prefer to appoint people in the shadow of their political careers as new British Commissioners rather than people who are mainstream politicians. Similarly, after retiring from Brussels, Britain's ex-Commissioners are never again utilised for their contacts and expert knowledge of how the Community works. The use of our retirees from Brussels has been tragically wasteful in comparison to what happens to the ex-Commissioners of other Community countries.

None of Britain's five ex-Commissioners since we joined in 1973 have been given jobs which used their European experience on returning to Britain. Christopher (now Lord) Soames returned from Brussels, joined Mrs. Thatcher's cabinet and was given responsibility for supervising the transition to independence of Zimbabwe, then became Minister for the Civil Service, and then was retired to the House of Lords. George (now Lord) Thomson chaired first the Advertising Standards Authority and subsequently the Independent Broadcasting Authority. Roy Jenkins struggled to return to the House of Commons in a new party. Christopher Tugendhat and Ivor Richard returned in January 1985 and were ignored. *None* of the five's expert knowledge of Europe was ever again employed by a British government for the benefit of the British people.

... UNLIKE THE CONTINENTALS

The continental approach could not be more different. In the same period since Britain joined in 1973, two of the three French ex-Commissioners left Brussels to join their national government at senior levels: Raymond Barre became Prime Minister under President Giscard d'Estaing; Claude Cheysson became Foreign Minister under President Mitterand. If the reason for this contrast in after-use is that the French send higher quality people to Brussels in the first place, that merely indicates how much more effectively they play the European game than the British.

The other eight member states also use their ex-Commissioners more effectively than the British. Since 1973, of the ex-Commissioners from the other eight member states, one is the President of Ireland, two became Foreign Ministers (Belgium and Italy), one became Ambassador in Spain advancing German interests in a country which was about to join the Community.

NO USE FOR BRITAIN'S EX-M.E.P.s EITHER

The utilisation of Britain's ex-M.E.P.s since 1973 has been equally feeble. Not one has been given a political responsibility for dealing with Europe. In the Labour party only one ex-M.E.P., Guy Barnett, was a member of the 1976-79 government: he became an Under Secretary in the Department of the Environment responsible for sport, recreation and water resources! For the Conservatives, Alex Fletcher went to the Scottish Office in 1979, and then to responsibility for corporate and consumer affairs at the Department of Trade and Industry. Another Conservative ex-M.E.P., the Earl of Mansfield, serviced successively in the Scottish and Northern Ireland offices. Another, Mrs. Fenner, became Parliamentary Secretary in the Ministry of Agriculture. In the 1984 European elections a number of British M.E.P.s, several distinguished, were defeated or retired. Their special knowledge has been ignored. Only one has been employed to deal directly with the Community: Adam Fergusson has been made a special advisor by the Foreign Office.

In sharp contrast, the French utilisation of their ex-Europeans is admirable. Their band of ex-M.E.P.s includes President Mitterand, plus the recent Prime Minister Mauroy and five other cabinet ministers. Similarly, in the eight other Community member states, ex-M.E.P.s have included two Prime Ministers (Italy and Luxembourg), three Foreign Ministers (Italy, Luxembourg, Belgium), two Agriculture Ministers (Belgium, Denmark), and five Ministers for Trade or Industry (France, Greece, Ireland, Belgium, Denmark). All know the Community system well and in most cases they know each other too. Sad to relate, since 1973 Lord Soames has been the only member of any British Cabinet who has had any first-hand experience of Europe (and even his was not used directly).

IS OUR ELECTORAL SYSTEM A VALID EXCUSE?
It might be argued that the British failure to use Euro-experience in our national government is due to the British electoral system—which necessitates the finding of a safe seat in the House of Commons for an ex-Commissioner or ex-M.E.P. and then a probably hazardous by-election. On first sight the British system of by-elections appears more hazardous for the government than the continental method of automatic replacement by the next name on the previous election's list of candidates. But in Britain we can create life peers and give them responsibility in government without their having to obtain a single vote. So we cannot use our peculiar electoral system as an excuse for our failure to use our people with European experience.

NO EXPERIENCE OF BRUSSELS FOR OUR CIVIL SERVANTS
In the same way, Britain's use of its civil servants in Whitehall and in Brussels is unsatisfactory. A small number of chosen highflying British civil servants are sent to Brussels on secondment. After a due period

they are brought back to Whitehall where their knowledge is used. But at lower levels, if an able or ambitious British civil servant wishes to gain European knowledge in order to advance his own prospects no help is given to him or her to go to Brussels—neither, if they wish to return, for them to subsequently resume their career to London. To obtain such experience they are obliged to resign from Whitehall and take their chance in Brussels with no re-entry facility back to London again. The consequence is that a number of people who could perform well in Brussels do not got there on behalf of Britain, and equally a number of good British people in Brussels are not able to return to the United Kingdom to use their knowledge for the benefit of the British public.

The use of French civil servants in and out of Brussels is far more productive for the benefit of the French people. It is a criteria of the French civil service that highfliers should do a spell in Brussels. After a period of working there, they are returned to Paris to use their knowledge.

ANOTHER ASPECT OF BRITISH WASTE: OUR ISOLATED CURRENCY

We have not joined the European Monetary System as full members. The System has become firmly established, contrary to our usual British scepticism. A House of Lords committee recommended that Britain should join as a full member in 1983. The Confederation of British Industry has called for Britain to join. Joining would provide stability for sterling, whose continual gyrations have hindered British importers and exporters. Sharp currency fluctuations hinder trade and economic growth. If we continue to opt out, we shall see the rules and the experience increasingly suit our partners rather than ourselves. Shall we never learn?

All these areas for improvement are a reflection of the lack of enthusiasm with which British governments regard our membership of the European Community. It is no wonder that the British people feel they do not get benefits from the Europe when their national leaders do not pull the strings sufficiently hard on their behalf.

AN POSITIVE INITIATIVE FROM BRITAIN IS LONG OVERDUE

Something positive from Britain is long overdue. Mrs. Thatcher did extremely well to press for more effective use of the Community's financial resources. This was necessary because few of the continental governments were willing to consider reforms seriously. She was right to insist that the foundations of united Europe are constructed securely.

But there has never been a single positive British initiative in the whole history of the Community. It would enormously assist Britain to win her arguments if Britain were to launch even one imaginative idea for European action *in a new area*. Recent initiatives have tended to be French—Esprit, Eureka, and so on. Without something positive from Britain, it is no wonder that, because of our consistently negative attitude, our partners genuinely believe that the British are seeking to destroy the Community or at least to reduce it to a free trade area only.

BRITISH BUSINESSMEN ARE NOT MUCH BETTER

Our businessmen should take a positive interest in the Community. Criticism does not rest solely on the House of Commons and on the government. Other sectors of activity in Britain have also neglected their opportunities. Too few British businessmen understand how to lobby in the Community, or know how to follow new developments in Brussels which will affect them in the future. Too few have even visited Brussels. There is still a belief among British businessmen that it is sufficient to lobby their Westminster M.P. about future European legislation! They are still unaware that a Westminster M.P. has no vote on European legislation, that it is a national minister who commits our country in the Council of Ministers, and that when the House of Commons subsequently debates what the minister has decided it only votes "to take note".

British businessmen consistently fail to obtain a due share of contracts from the European Development Fund (known as the E.D.F.) compared to other large member states. The E.D.F. exists to channel Community financial aid to developing countries. Under its rules, the developing countries must select a Community company to carry out each contract which is paid by the E.D.F. Yet from the Fourth Fund (by the end of 1983), British companies had won only 14.4 per cent of the contracts by value—against 33.7 per cent for French companies and 19 per cent for German companies. From the Fifth E.D.F. Fund British companies had won only 15.9 per cent against 34.1 per cent to the French and 23.8 per cent to the Germans. If British companies achieved a proportionate share of these contracts there would be more jobs in Britain.

WE MUST BE WILLING TO LEARN FROM OUR COMMUNITY PARTNERS

There are deep problems within our own country, and it is not impossible that we might be able to learn something helpful occasionally about solving them from our partners. The attitude of the House of Commons was appallingly negative and hostile when the European Parliament decided to study the problem of Northern Ireland in view of the money that the Community spends there. If one's friends are willing to try to help, the least one can do is to listen to their opinion. As things turned out, the European Parliament's report was helpful to the British position.

THE CONFRONTATIONAL HABIT EXAMPLE OF THE HOUSE OF COMMONS

A particular British problem is the confrontational attitude that exists within our country. The divide between "us and them", management and unions, left and right, is more intense and divisive than in parts of the continent. How do they do it? Should we not be willing to find out? It is possible to speculate that the divisions within our country are aggravated by the confrontational attitude within the House of Commons. The attitudes of different groups of opinion in our country cannot be improved by the constant sight of two opposing armies which hurl insults at each other across the chamber of the House of Commons each day, and vow to reverse each other's policies as soon as possible. The chambers of parliaments in most parts of the world are horseshoe shaped so that all members face the Speaker and not their enemy.

OUR ELECTORAL SYSTEM PRODUCES UNHELPFUL DISTORTIONS

Another British problem is our present electoral system which is fair only when there are only two parties; currently it produces disproportionate results in national and in European elections, and leads to under-representation in important areas of our society. Have our national legislators the courage to learn from systems which are successful elsewhere in the European Community?

Critics of proportional representation in Britain try, by taking selective examples, to argue that it would be damaging to introduce any proportional system into Britain. It is easy to select bad examples of proportional representation—the instability of Italian politics is a prime example because they have too many minority parties. But other forms of voting systems can be shown to be superior in the results that they produce compared to the British system. The system in the Federal Republic of Germany was imposed by the British after the Second

World War. It combines proportionality with constituencies. It has a "five per cent threshold" rule, so that splinter parties which fail to win five per cent of the total vote obtain no seats. Germany has consequently experienced fewer changes of leader and fewer changes of administration that has Britain since 1945 and has not suffered from our extreme swings of the pendulum between right and left.

The Irish, both North and South, use the single transferable vote combined with the direct constituency link, which is another attractive combination.

CONTINENTALS ARE BETTER AT ENCOURAGING SMALL BUSINESSES

Our Conservative government's efforts to improve the climate for the creation of new jobs has not been effective enough. In 1983 the European Parliament commissioned a study of the climate for the profitability of Small Businesses in each of the ten member states of the Community.

The shocking conclusion for the British was that our country was graded as second worst for small businesses! The report showed that it is best to be operating a small business in Germany—and then, in deteriorating order, in Greece, France, Netherlands, Denmark, Belgium, Luxembourg, Ireland and Britain. Only in Italy is the climate worse for small businesses than in Britain!

Britain's conditions for small business were graded as best in the Community in only one way, taxation. We are worst in productivity growth, costs of premises, subsidised lending, and protection against monopolies. Will Westminster be willing to learn from Europe that we have an enormous amount of ground to catch up if our smaller businesses are to spawn the hundreds of thousands of new jobs that we desperately require?

THE GOVERNMENT COULD BE BRAVER IN HELPING BUSINESS

There have been examples where the British government has taken the easy way out instead of helping Britain to become competitive. When the Community decided to move a little nearer to having a common market by harmonising the maximum weight of lorries, the European Parliament's recommendation of forty tons was accepted—but not by Britain. Our maximum in Britain is to be less, only thirty-eight tons. No lorries will be manufactured which only carry thirty-eight tons: every lorry manufacturer will design for the much larger forty ton market. Consequently, assuming that all truck drivers will obey the law,

Britain now has slightly higher transport costs per ton than our competitors on the continent—with negative consequences for employment in Britain.

THE URGENT NEED TO IMPROVE PUBLIC UNDERSTANDING ABOUT HOW THE COMMUNITY WORKS

The government has a duty to create a better understanding by the British public of how the European Community works. Too many people are unaware that the European Parliament is their only way to democratically control events. Too few people realise that myopic nationalism has deprived them of the anticipated benefits from our membership. When people in Britain blame things on the Community, they demonstrate that they are incapable of distinguishing between the different institutions of the Community. They are unaware that almost all the blame for the failures belongs to the inability to take decisions by the national members of the Council of Ministers. The Commission and the European Parliament have almost always done their job and carried out their responsibilities efficiently. But the public has never been told that it is their *national* ministers who have failed them and not the Community as a whole, nor the Commission nor the Euro-M.P.s. A very much greater level of understanding and awareness about the workings of Europe are necessary, in order that the British people may exercise their influence and shape the future development of Europe.

The public must be helped to understand that the Community is still far from complete, that its future is uncertain, and that the major obstacle to its success is too much nationalism.

It may be encouraging to glance at the history of the United States of America. Disputes raged for sixty years between supporters of Jefferson and the Federalists: the Federalists believed that the Union was the expression of the common interest but that it would never become anything if the interests of the Union did not predominate over those of the individual states. For as long as decisions had to be made unanimously, there was little progress: but progress accelerated when decisions began to be taken by majority votes. If the American federalists finally won their argument, why should not also the Europeans?

If those who believe in a united Europe try hard enough, and persist for long enough, to adapt the words of the famous American poet Walt Whitman, they will see Europe "can at last become what it is".

CHAPTER NINE

Who Is Afraid Of A United States Of Europe?

The logical goal of an "ever closer union" between the peoples of Europe is the creation of a federal European system—such as exists in other large areas of the world including the U.S.A., Canada and Australia. This might be called something like a "United States of Europe".

The many potential advantages to the British people of living in a federal Europe have not been discussed in Britain.

If our descendants lived in a federal Europe they would have more opportunities, more freedom and more prosperity. They would be free to travel, to settle, and to work anywhere they wanted in Europe—just as Americans already can in their own continent. They would have to endure fewer governmental and bureaucratic controls—no customs and passport delays at internal frontiers, no residence permits, no currency restrictions, no having to change money at each internal border.

A federal Europe was the dream of Winston Churchill. Even in 1942 during the war he was writing privately to Anthon Eden: "My thoughts rest primarily in Europe . . . It would be a measureless disaster if Russian barbarism overlaid the culture and independence of the ancient states of Europe . . . Hard as it is to say now, I trust that the European family may act unitedly as one . . . I look forward to a United States of Europe . . ."

Our descendants in a federal Europe would be safer—because their defence would be organised with less of the rivalry and duplication that exists at present between the different nation states of Europe: they would have standardised (and therefore cheaper) weapons and ammunition instead of the different ones in different countries, as we have now.

Unemployment would be lower than it is now and they would be more prosperous than we are now. The U.S.A. has a lower rate of unemployment than Europe because it is a single market from coast to coast. Also the Americans do not have the disadvantage that present-day Europeans endure—that about seven per cent of the value of our manufactured goods is spent on getting them past the delays at the internal frontier controls which exist between our different states: the abolition of internal border controls would mean cheaper goods, therefore more trade, therefore more jobs, and therefore more prosperity.

Drugs and terrorists would be combatted better than at present: currently each little nation state adopts its own individual measures against drug traffickers and terrorists; the efforts of present-day European police forces are not sufficiently coordinated.

Rabies could still be kept out of Britain: Denmark is currently free of rabies even though it is linked by land to the continent.

Of course there would be difficulties in getting to a United States of Europe. We have too many languages in Europe: perhaps three—say English, French and Spanish—would have to become the major official ones.

Would we lose our British sovereignty? Yes, but we have lost most of it already. The pound sterling goes up and down like a yo-yo; disarmament is discussed at Geneva without us; our forces are under the orders of an American general in N.A.T.O. Instead of this, a federal Europe would give us a share of a European sovereignty which would be stronger and more real than our present limited and shrinking British sovereignty.

The House of Commons would continue to exist—being there to decide the usual things that purely concern the British, just as California and Texas in the U.S.A. have their own state Legislatures.

So, who is afraid of a United States of Europe? The answer is "Britain's *national* politicians". They enjoy pretending that they are still in charge of Britain's destiny: in practice however they are able to achieve much less because outside pressures from world events play an increasing part in our affairs. The fear of our national politicians is that a federal Europe would downgrade their apparent importance. Therefore they will not discuss it—and therefore the public never hears about the idea.

Surely the idea of a United States of Europe is worth discussing by the British? It might even prove to be the best prospect that we can offer to the future generations who will come after us.

INDEX

Acheson, Dean	17, 68
Agriculture—see	
Common Agricultural Policy	
Aid	10, 21
Air	34, 39, 46
Airbus	34
Alliance parties	70
Architects	37, 44
Argentina	46-47, 64
Ariane	34
Asia	23
Australia	59, 81
Austria	8, 15, 30
Austria-Hungary	18
Barre, Raymond	74
Barnett, Guy	74
Basques	61
Beef	13
Belgium	28, 39, 44, 58, 61, 74, 75, 79
Bevin, Ernest	27
Briand	24
Budget	47, 51, 52, 69, 70
Bundestag	71-72
Butter	13, 38, 69
Canada	59, 81
Catherwood, Sir Fred	43
Castle, Barbara	69
Cereals	13, 44, 49
C.E.R.N.	34
Chelsea F.C.	31
Cheysson, Claude	74
China	22
Churchill, Winston	24-28, 68, 81
Clinton Davis, Stanley	50
Coal and Steel	28
Cockfield, Lord	50

Commission	36, 39, 40, 42, 50, 53, 54, 56, 80
Commissioners	50, 73
Common Agricultural Policy	10-12, 18, 32, 44, 46, 51, 52, 54, 59, 72
Common Market	8, 18, 22, 29, 44, 58
Commons, House of	36, 51, 58, 67, 71, 72, 74, 77, 78, 82
Commonwealth	8, 27
Computers	33
Confederation of British Industry	76
Conservative Party	13, 56, 58, 59, 66, 70, 74
Constituencies	69, 79
Council of Europe	27, 28, 62
Council of Ministers	36-42, 46, 50, 51, 53, 54, 56, 72, 77, 80
Couve de Murville	41
C.S.C.E.	53
Currencies	19, 44, 59, 65, 76, 81
Customs	31, 39, 43, 53, 66, 81
Czechoslovakia	61
Defence	20, 28, 29, 57, 59, 60, 65, 81
Democratic Gap	50-54
Denmark	30, 39, 44, 57, 58, 75, 79, 82
Developing Countries	10, 77
Drugs	82
East Germany	61
E.C.U.	32, 44
Eden, Sir Anthony	25, 29, 81
Education	44
Electoral Reform	45, 70, 78-79
E.S.P.R.I.T.	33, 37, 77
Ethiopia	13
Eureka	77
European Army	28

European Atomic
  Energy Community   29-30
European Convention on
  Human Rights   28, 61, 65
European Court of Justice 36, 37, 48-49
European Defence Community   29
European Development Fund   77
European Free Trade Area 8, 30, 61, 77
European Monetary System 32, 44, 76
European Parliament 31-33, 36-38, 40,
    43, 44, 47-51, 53-54, 56, 57,
    59, 60, 66, 72,
    73, 78-80
Exports   7-9

Falklands   46
Federalism   57, 59, 80-82
Fenner, Mrs. Peggy   75
Fergusson, Adam   75
Finland   8, 15, 30
Fisheries   33, 44
FitzGerald, Dr. Garret   37
Fletcher, Alex   74
Folketing   72
Fontáinebleau Summit 48, 66, 73
Food   8, 12
Foreign Affairs   10, 59, 71
France 9, 11, 18, 20, 24, 28, 39, 41, 44,
    57, 64, 75, 76, 79
Freedom   7, 13, 31, 81
Frontiers   19

G.A.T.T.   53, 64
Gaulle, General De 30, 32, 41, 42
Genscher   48
Germany 9, 18, 22, 28, 39, 44, 45, 58,
    61, 74, 78, 79
Gibraltar   61
Giscard d'Estaing   74
Greece 11, 31, 39, 44, 57, 61, 75, 79
Gross National Product   9, 21

Hugo, Victor   24
Hungary   61

Iceland   30, 33
Identity Cards   63

Inflation   19
India   22, 62
Indonesia   22
Insurance   44, 46
Investment   13
Ireland, Republic of 20, 30, 39, 44,
    47, 61, 74, 75, 79
Italy 11, 18, 28, 39, 44, 45, 47, 58, 64,
    74, 75, 78, 79

Japan   8-10, 13, 20, 22, 45
Jefferson   80
Jenkins, Roy   74
Jobs   10, 43, 79, 81
Joint European Torus   33

Karamanlis   22
Kohl, Helmut   58
Korea, South   28, 44

Labour Party 8, 14, 58, 70, 74, 78
Languages   36, 61, 62, 82
League of Nations   45
Liechtenstein   14
Lomé Convention   31
Lords, House of   71, 74, 76
Lorries   54, 79
Luxembourg 28, 39, 41, 44, 75, 79
Luxembourg Compromise   42, 48

Macmillan, Harold   30
Majority Voting   38-39, 70
Mansfield, Earl of   75
Manufacturing Decline   9
Mauroy, Pierre   75
M.E.P.s 33, 38, 47, 58, 66, 69, 72, 73
  ex-M.E.P.s   71, 74-75
Messina Conference   29
Milan Summit   57
Milk   11, 38, 44, 63, 73
Mitterand, Francois 46, 48, 57, 74, 75
Monetary Union   57
Monarchy   60, 63
Monnet, Jean   28-29
Morocco   61
Motorcars   8, 10, 35

Napoleon	11	Spinelli, Altiero	56, 58
Nation State	19-21	Steel	44
N.A.T.O.	15, 20, 61, 65, 82	Stresemann	24
Netherlands	18, 28, 39, 45, 64, 79	Stuttgart Summit	56
Northern Ireland	45, 58, 61, 78, 79	Subsidiarity	60
Norway	8, 15, 30-31	Subsidies	12, 54
Nuclear Energy	29, 30, 33	Suez	65
		Sugar	31
O.E.C.C.	27, 45	Surpluses	13
O.E.C.D.	28, 45	Sweden	8, 15, 30, 33
Oil	8, 65	Switzerland	8, 15, 30, 33, 59
O.P.E.C.	64, 65		
		Tariffs	9
		Terrorists	82
Paris, Treaty of	28	Thatcher, Mrs. Mararet	48, 50, 54, 56, 66, 70, 71, 74, 76
Passports	19, 35, 43, 66, 81		
Perfidious Albion	47	Thomson, Lord	74
Petain	24	Tornado	34
Plumb, Sir Henry	69	Trade Unions	14
Poland	48, 61	Transport	39, 48, 80
Population	12, 21	Tugendhat, Christopher	74
Portugal	11, 15, 31, 39, 44	Turkey	30, 61
Proportional Representation	45, 70, 78		
		Unemployment	19, 43, 81
Rabies	63, 82	United Nations	4, 27, 28, 45
Rebate	47, 66, 69, 70, 72-73	United States of America	8-10, 12, 13, 18, 20-22, 24, 52, 59, 80-82
Regional Development Fund	32, 44		
Representatives, House of	52, 69	United States of Europe	24-26, 29, 34, 58, 81-82
Richard, Ivor	74		
Rome, Treaty of	13, 29, 37-39, 42, 51, 55, 56, 59	U.S.S.R.	15, 18, 19, 21, 25
Roosevelt	26	V.A.T.	66, 71
		Venice Conference	29
Savary, Alain	18	Vetoes	32, 37-51, 58, 69
Schuman, Robert	28		
S.D.P.	58	Westminster	60, 66, 67, 69, 70
Senate, U.S.	52, 60	Western European Union	29
Small Business	79	Whitman, Walt	80
Soames, Lord	74-75	Wilson, Harold	30
Social Fund	31, 39	Withdrawal	11
Soccer	31, 65		
Sovereignty	62-66, 82	Yaounde	31
Spaak, Paul-Henri	29	Yugoslavia	61
Space Research	34		
Spain	11, 15, 20, 31, 39, 44, 61, 74	Zimbabwe	74